THE RAILWAY POLICE

THE
RAILWAY POLICE

NIGEL WIER

authorHOUSE®

AuthorHouse™
1663 Liberty Drive
Bloomington, IN 47403
www.authorhouse.com
Phone: 1-800-839-8640

First published by AuthorHouse   09/24/2011

ISBN: 978-1-4670-0026-0 (sc)
ISBN: 978-1-4670-0027-7 (ebk)

Printed in the United States of America

CONTENTS

For Angie of course

For my son, Alex

For my parents, Albert and Maisie

For Martha and in memory of Harry

PROLOGUE

This book is about the history of The Railway Police or The British Transport Police (BTP) as they are now known as. The Railway Police began its life or its history many years ago in 1826, making it probably the oldest police force of its kind in the United Kingdom, and over the years it has been known by many a different name, but its role has always been the same to look after the policing of the railways, the docks, the ports, the canals and at some stage even the London buses.

Although in the book I state that I am dealing with the history of the railway police that is strictly not true, although I do deal with their history many parts of the book will also refer to the work that they do on a daily basis, so yes I suppose that would be classed as part of their history. I have outlined some of the horrific and difficult crimes that go on throughout the railway structure, from murders, suicides, terror attacks all the way though to robberies, thefts, public order, trespassing and other offences that they are expected to deal with.

You cannot write about the history of the railway police without mentioning the crime that they deal with because as you will see from the book whatever crimes or whatever incidents that occur in a public street or roadway they most certainly will happen on the railway to.

They are called upon to deal with any crime that takes place either over ground or underground. So yes it is about their history but it is also about their work.

And you will see from the last chapter in the book that many railway police have lost their lives. As of 2011 there had been thirty one such reported deaths, this information is direct from the British Transport Police themselves and it is hoped that the list is correct and up to date, but the British Transport Police Roll of Honour is on-going work and what has to be appreciated is that since the formation of the first railway police all those many years ago, there have been many amalgamations of different railway forces, and over those years there is always a feeling that some records of deaths and possibly murders and the associated paperwork and details may have been lost forever.

What I hope is that when people have finished reading this book they will realise that the police who are responsible for policing the railways are a very important police force and they most certainly add to the security and safety of this country and its people.

ACKNOWLEDGEMENTS

I must firstly thank the British Transport Police themselves as they have allowed me to use their very formative web site for most of my research into the history of the railway police, in particular I would like to thank the Media and Marketing Department of the BTP for their support and assistance when I had urgent or perhaps even difficult questions to ask and that I needed answers for.

Never once have they let me down they have always been very quick and very positive in their responses to me and have actively encouraged me in the writing of the book.

Nigel Wier

I would also like to thank Birmingham Central Library Archives Department for their patience and understanding during my regular visits.

There are other people I would like to thank for the writing of this book but they have to remain anonymous but they of course will know who they are.

There may be omissions and errors within the book and I apologise now beforehand but there are certainly without malice on the part of the author.

ABBREVIATIONS

PC	Police Constable
DC	Detective Constable
Sgt	Sergeant
PS	Police Sergeant
DS	Detective Sergeant
DI	Detective Inspector
DCI	Detective Chief Inspector
D/Supt	Detective Superintendent
DCS	Detective Chief Superintendent
CC	Chief Constable
SC	Special Constable

Peeler	Policeman
Bobby	Policeman
CID	Criminal Investigation Department
BTCP	British Transport Commission Police
BTP	British Transport Police
STO	Sexually Trained Officer
NPT	Neighbourhood Policing Team
SIO	Senior Investigating Officer
ACPO	Association of Chief Police Officers
CCTV	Close Circuit Television
HQ	Headquarters
TUC	Trades Union Congress
OBE	Order of the British Empire
CBE	Command of the British Order
QPM	Queens Police Medal
PIRA	Provisionally Irish Republic Army

CHAPTER ONE
THE BEGINNING

The Railway Police or on various occasions throughout this book I will refer to them as they are now known as either the British Transport Police or BTP for short. They can trace their history back as far as 1826 making them potential the oldest police force in the country and of course not the Metropolitan Police who people always assumed were the oldest, in actual fact they did not begin their existence until 1829 so the railway police pre-date them by at least three years.

How can we prove that fact? Well a regulation in the book of rules of the Stockton and Darlington Railway refers to the police establishment of 1826 as one Superintendent, four officers and numerous gate keepers; this is the first mention of the railway police of any description anywhere and is three years before the Metropolitan Police Act was passed and indeed the formation of the Metropolitan Police.

They were never referred to as Constables and I suppose the description could mean they were controlling and looking after the railways and rolling stock and not enforcing the law and protecting the people out on the street. That unfortunately is a something I do not think we will ever know as I am sure that they would have been used for both roles if and when they were needed.

Now first things first, the Stockton and Darlington Railway was opened in 1825, it was 26 miles long and was built between Witton Park, Stockton on Tees and it ended in Darlington, it stopped at several collieries along the way, it steadily expanded serving both South and West Durham, Cleveland and Westmorland and was eventually taken over by North Eastern Railway in 1863. The brief history lesson is over with for the time being.

So that is why I believe that the railway police were in fact the first police force however small at the time and was the first of its kind anywhere in this country. There is no doubt that some of the historians of the Metropolitan Police will disagree.

The Railway Police

The Metropolitan Police Act 1829 changed an awful lot, it was firstly an Act of Parliament, nothing before that ever was, and it was introduced by Sir Robert Peel and passed by the Parliament of the United Kingdom of the day, the act established the Metropolitan Police district except for the City of London or Inner London as it was also known as.

This replaced the previous parish constables and watchmen and gate keepers. The Act enabled legislation for what is considered the first modern police force of its kind and the policemen were often referred to as 'bobbies' or 'peelers' after the founder Sir Robert Peel.

So I suppose the dispute of who is the oldest police force in the country will continue for some time yet and for a lot of people.

Of course when the first of Sir Robert Peels 'peelers' or 'bobbies' were walking the streets of London, railways were already in existence, as for the first Railway Act ever found is dated 1758 but in those days' railways were used to carry goods only and not passengers and only for a short distance and horsepower provided the locomotion for the trains.

In 1830 the Liverpool and Manchester Railway was formally opened by the Duke of Wellington, it was the first public railway in the world to carry both goods and passengers, however on the first occasion it was used it was also marred by the first known railway fatality.

The Right Honourable William Huskisson disobeyed the railway companies' instruction of not getting off the train track side and he proceeded to do just that and got off the train track side and stepped onto a second track and was struck by a passing train and killed.

As far as is known that was the first recorded fatality involving a train.

There was a large crowd present to watch proceedings to see the very first train used for both passengers and goods anywhere in the world let alone the United Kingdom, and it caused public order difficulties throughout the day and the obvious need for railway police was there for all to see, as a report on the day of the fatality recorded the following quotation, 'the local garrison was under arms at various points within the sight of the railway, cavalry were also placed'

So without the military presence there would certainly have been a breach of the peace, in other words the army had been used to police the railways surely that was never right. This would need to change very quickly and it did.

CHAPTER TWO
THE FIRST RAILWAY POLICE

So within a few months of both the Metropolitan Police Act 1829 and the opening of the Liverpool and Manchester Railway in 1830 the first railway police were to be formed.

In November 1830 minutes taken from the Liverpool and Manchester Railway refer to, 'The Police Establishment' and less than a year later it is satisfactory to note that a pay rise was given to the railway police due to the responsibility of their office.

These early railway police were probably sworn in as special constables under a statute passed in 1673 during the reign of Charles II of England; they would certainly not have been passed under the Act of Parliament that gave us the Metropolitan Police Act 1929.

They were appointed to.

1. Preserve law and order on the construction site of the railway.
2. Patrol and protect the line.
3. Control the movement of railway traffic.
4. To this end, station houses were placed at one mile intervals along the line to provide shelter for the railway police, the term police station used by most police forces today probably would have originated from these buildings or station houses.

So were the railway police of 1830 very much different to the reference made by the regulation of the Stockton and Darlington Railway of 1826 when they refer to the police establishment I think probably not.

The Railway Companion of 1833 referred directly to the Liverpool and Manchester Railway by saying, 'the company keeps a police establishment who have station houses at intervals about a mile apart along the road, these stations form depots for passengers and goods from or to any intervening place. The duties assigned to these men are to guard the road, to prevent or give notice of any obstruction and to render assistance in the case of any accident occurring and to do so effectively and to keep up a continued line of communication.'

The above came into force because of the Special Constables Act 1831.

Now remember we have already said that the railway police were probably sworn in as special constables, and the passing of the above act said that railway policeman had jurisdiction not only on the railway but in the area in which they were appointed, the London, Birmingham and Liverpool Companion of 1838 stated, 'each constable besides being in the employment of the company is sworn as a county constable.'

What that meant is that they, the railway police would receive the same pay of a constable with the Metropolitan Police, they would wear a similar uniform except the colour the railway police uniform would be green.

Their hats were similar almost like a top hat in style, and in order to regulate the trains the railway police were issued with watches, flags and lamps, the Ulster Railway Police were even issued with a shovel and a wheelbarrow to remove rubbish or obstructions from the railway lines.

The watch was a rare item among the working man at the time and was used to ensure there was a suitable time delay between trains entering each section of track and leaving each section of track thereby hopefully avoiding any sort of collision. They also had two flags a red one for trains to 'stop' and a white flag meaning 'all clear'

The duties of the railway police or forerunners to the police service as we know it were to maintain law and order on the railways and to regulate the movement of trains, these somewhat static and in the main routine duties were to change as in the next fifty years the railway system as we know it was to extend throughout the country, so the duties of the railway police were going to have to extend as well.

CHAPTER THREE
THE NAVVIES

The navvies as they were more commonly known were to become the very huge work force that was going to be needed to build and maintain the ever expanding railway system, which would be stretching around the country and into every corner of the country.

Thousands and thousands of men that had previously been used to cut canals or navigations were now being used to build stations, lay railway track, dig cuttings, build up embankments and of course excavate tunnels. These men were effectually known as 'navvies' I wonder if this word came from the word navigations, which is something that they were previously involved in doing.

These men came in the main from Ireland, Wales, and Scotland and some even as far afield as the continent, because they needed the work whatever the pay and the railways needed them to work on the ever expanding railway system, so it soon became an ideal relationship.

But these men, the navvies was not something that the pleasant, rural and genteel Victorian folk of England knew much about or indeed wanted to know much about, but they learnt quick as large shanty towns were being built in rural areas to accommodate these men who of course all required food and water and other home comforts. These armies of rough people bought with them naturally their hangers on.

And what is a shanty town, well it is another word for a 'squat' or a 'squatter settlement' more at home in impoverished countries not lovely Victorian England, anyway it is basically a slum type of settlement made from any of sort of material you could find, wood metal and stuff like that and most probably none of the shanty towns had proper sanitation or running water.

But what they did have was a large crowd of men who wanted to work hard and probably play hard, and who would work for a few pennies and I suppose they should be referred to as railway workers and not navvies.

Of note in 1836 the inhabitants of Buckinghamshire asked the newly formed Metropolitan Police to send some of their police officers to protect them from these men building the railways, they believed their own parochial constable would be totally unable to afford them any protection. The request apparently was declined by the Metropolitan Police.

An early account of these railway workers said of them, 'they injured everything they approached' in other words they tore down fences, trees, plantation, flowers, hedges, animals disappeared, game disappeared, game keepers were defied, they ruined corn fields and the inhabitants felt imprisoned by the hundreds of invading railway workers.

Something had to happen and it did.

The Local Justices appointed special constables to help keep the invading army of railway workers or navvies under control, but the cost of this of course fell onto the local ratepayer, so in consequence on 10th August 1838 an Act was passed which required the railway companies who of course employed the railway workers, to pay for the constables to keep the peace near and by all railway work under construction.

However these newly appointed constables certainly had their work cut out looking after these railway workers and quite often could not themselves cope with the disorder that was caused by them, and in 1830 when the Chester and Birkenhead Railway was being constructed and fighting broke out between the English and the Irish navvies, a detachment of the local infantry were called in to quell the disorder and in took four days before some sort of peace was restored.

CHAPTER FOUR
BATTLE OF MICKLETON

But the problems continued and really there were always going to be problems, potential trouble and fighting because when you have got hundreds of people of all races, Irish, English, Scottish, Welsh and from many continental countries, and you were expecting them all to work in some sort of harmony and then of course expecting them to live together as one big happy family, I am afraid it was never going to happen, they are of course only human.

In 1840 labourers murdered a railway ganger, the ganger being the head or the foreman of a group of labourers, on the partly constructed Edinburgh to Glasgow Railway line and it required a company, some 200 men of the 58th Foot

Infantry to find and arrest the ring leaders of the murder. A make shift scaffold was put together at the side of the railway track very quickly and the perpetrators were subsequently hanged without trial.

But so the disorder continued and in 1846, two navvies were arrested for stealing watches from other railway workers and placed in a lock up near to Edinburgh, several other navvies marched to the police house where they forcibly released the two prisoners and then they proceeded to bludgeon to death the local constable, PC Richard Pace

In Swindon the same year navvies tunnelled under the floor of a lock up to release one of their arrested friends.

In 1851 even the great Isambard Kingdom Brunel probably the world's greatest engineer and of course engineer of the Great Western Railway became involved in these so called disorders amongst the navvies. He was involved in what became the 'Battle of Mickleton' which is thought by historians to be the last battle fought by private armies on British soil.

The opening of the Oxford, Worcester and Wolverhampton railway line southward from Evesham had been delayed and the cause of the problem appeared to be the construction of the Mickleton tunnel near to Chipping Camden, not by fighting this time but by floods causing large land slips and mud to collect and build up by the entrance to the tunnel making it virtually impossible to work on.

In 1846 Brunel employed a new contractor but by 1849 it had solved nothing and any further work on the tunnel was suspended.

In 1851 the company headed by its chief engineer, Brunel decided to take possession of the plant and machinery and arrange for a new contractor to come in. The old contractor who stated that he was owed a large amount of money by the company, the Oxford, Worcester and Wolverhampton Railway decided to stay put and defied them.

The contractor even got two local magistrates to attend at the scene as he expected a fight with Brunel, the Riot Act was read and the matter was put off and the men dispersed. But the following day Brunel arrived back with his army of navvies estimated to be 3000 strong because they wanted to work and they were faced with the contractor with his army of men, plus the local constables from Chipping Camden, because the contractor was in dispute over money and was not allowing any work to take place.

So the Battle of Mickleton commenced, Brunel's men and the contractors men and local police, several heads and limbs were damaged, bones were broken but nobody seems to have been killed and with little resistance left the contractor agreed to give in and he and Brunel adjourned and came to an amicable agreement. So the battle was over before the arrival of troops from Coventry had got there.

A new contractor was appointed and the Mickleton tunnel was eventually finished without further violence or disruption in the spring of 1852.

The use of special constables on the railways in an attempt to quell the trouble was not unusual, as quite often railway employees themselves were sworn in as special constables and the beauty of special constables is that they were paid for by the railway companies, it was hoped that it would make the companies more responsible.

In 1846 such towns as Crewe, Slough and Swindon which were purpose built towns to accommodate the railway workers in the continuing construction of the railways were actually policed by the railway companies police themselves, and in 1846 the first police station of its kind was built in Crewe by the railway company and it also appointed all the officers who worked from there.

CHAPTER FIVE
CHANGING ROLE

But the role of the railway police was changing all the time, there was the advent of mechanical signalling and the invention of the first electric telegraph, which of course meant for the railway police less and less of their time was now line side or trackside and they were now expected to do much more.

Then with the introduction of county police forces under the County Police Act 1839 and 1840 and borough police forces under the County and Borough Police Act 1856, what this actually meant in real terms was that under an Act of Parliament it was compulsory for a police force to be established in any county that had not previously formed one.

In total there were 293 such forces, many of course were completely inadequate likes of course parts of the railway police.

So to the railway police were now or could be called upon to prevent and deal with crime on the railways and to assist with any other station duties, as the county and borough police forces were figuratively speaking expected to deal with all crime and disorder outside of the railway stations, so the railway police at this time had no reason whatsoever to step outside the confines of the railway station that was to be policed by the new county and borough police forces.

But the numbers of railway policemen were always increasing as and when new railway companies were formed, for an example when the Great Western Railway was finally opened by 1835, they had a police force which consisted of a Superintendent based at Paddington and under his command he had a total of 707 men.

Later in 1838 when the first section of the London to Southampton Railway line was opened, a written account stated, 'Policemen were more numerous than any other class of railway servant, they acted as signalmen and ticket collectors and were stationed along the line in their uniform of dark trousers, a swallow tailed coat and a tall hat with a leather crest.'

An 1837 Regulation of the Liverpool and Manchester Railway required that all intended passengers had to apply to a 'constable' for a ticket, but to give the constable 24 hours' notice, the passenger was also required to furnish the constable with his full name, address, place and date of birth or age, occupation and the reason for the journey and this was all written in the constables note book.

This of course was the forerunner for the term 'booking office' if the constable believed that the journey was lawful, he would issue a ticket and if not or he was not sure then he would not issue such a ticket. So now the railway police or constable who worked on the railway was now spending more of his time investigating crime and attempting to prevent crime it, in the first place and this subsequent course of action was hoped to go some way in reducing or even preventing that crime.

In 1838 a decision was made to transport all of Her Majesty's mail by the railway system for the first time ever, so the predictable occurred when within a short space of time mail thefts were reported, in 1848 the Eastern Counties Railway had 76 pieces of luggage or mail stolen in one day and the thefts from the main six operators in one year alone amounted to over £100,000.

Recorded by the Goods Manager at Euston Railway Station is that 'thieves are pilfering the goods from our wagons to an impudent extent, not a night passes without wine hampers, silk parcels, drapers boxes or other provisions being robbed' thefts of goods of course were often stolen by the railway employees themselves and in 1873 ten railway workers were sentenced to 10 years hard labour for stealing property from the railway from they worked.

As claims for compensation grew for the goods stolen or lost the railway companies decided to act by forming detective departments, the London and North Western Railway and Great Western Railway formed their CID in 1863, but both companies had previous to this used police officers in plain clothes to undertake special duties for several years before so it was not totally new to these companies but now it was made more official in its title.

Writing in 1894 the great historian John Pendleton said of the CID, 'the men in the detective departments on the railway do not fall like the persons they track, into disgrace. They are patient, enduring, and smart and sometimes do clever and important work that has more money value to the company'

The Railway Police

So the CID or Criminal Investigation Department on the railway was well up and running. But with more railways you had to have more crime one follows the other and some of this crime was serious crime such as murder or robbery.

CHAPTER SIX
JOHN TAWELL

On 1st January 1845, John Tawell was the first man to be arrested as a result of the use of the commercial electric telegraph on the railway system.

This particular telegraph was co-developed by Sir William Fothergill Cooke and Charles Wheatsone and it first entered commercial use in 1839 on the Great Western Railway covering an area of 13 miles from Paddington Railway Station to West Drayton Railway Station.

John Tawell was born in 1784 and during his early years worked in several different shops in London owned by the Quakers, he then married at 22 to a local girl called

Mary and he began to work in a chemist shop in Cheapside, London.

In 1814 at the age of 30 years he committed his first crime when he attempted to forge a £10 note, at this time forgery was a capital offence and when he appeared at court and was found guilty he was sentenced to death, however the victims of his crime were in fact Smiths Bank in London, and they were themselves Quakers and they naturally were bitterly opposed to the death penalty so luckily for Tawell, instead of death he was sentenced to transportation to the colonies for 14 years.

He ended up in Australia and his knowledge of medicine was soon identified in his new found country and he decided to set up a small local shop selling drugs and chemicals. He did well, made money and prospered and so much so he bought himself some land and in 1823 his wife and two children joined him from England.

He became well respected in the community and even wore the clothes of a Quaker including the wide brimmed hat. However in 1831 John Tawell and his family for some unknown reason decided to return to London, but this was 1830s London there was a high crime rate, it was also extremely heavily polluted and the atmosphere was extremely poor and of course it was one of the largest and most congested cities in the world.

The Railway Police

Bad luck would soon arrive for John Tawell and his wife as both of their young sons died within a short space of time, not helped of course by the polluted city that they had now chosen to live in. He was quite naturally heartbroken and his bad luck continued because in 1838 his wife Mary became very ill, so Tawell had no option he decided to employ the services of a young nurse to look after her.

Sarah Lawrence was her name, however late in 1838 his wife's condition became worse and despite constant attention and medication she too also died.

John Tawell was now a lonely and broken man with no family so he then began an affair with Sarah Lawrence and this relationship also bore the couple two children. Tawell then moved his lover who had now changed her name to Sarah Hart to an area known as Salt Hill, near Slough; he made regular visits to see her and the two children and he paid her £1 a week for the upkeep of the children.

By 1843 Tawell was beginning to experience more and more financial difficulties, and he thought that one means of relief from this debt would be the disposal of the financial burden of Sarah Hart, even though it was only £1 a week. On 1st January 1845 he went to a chemist and bough two bottles of Steele's acid, the acid was used for the treatment of varicose veins and contained poison prussic acid, he went to Paddington Station where he caught a train to Slough. He arrived in Slough and found Sarah in good spirits and they went to a local inn to buy a bottle of stout to share and returned home,

We do not really know what happened next but a short while later her next door neighbour heard loud shouting, groans and moans coming from Sarah's house, the neighbour looked out of the front window and saw Mr Tawell who she knew well leave Sarah's house and walk off. The neighbour went round to the house to see if she was alright, but instead found her writhing on the floor and frothing from the mouth, a doctor was summoned but by the time he arrived Sarah Hart was dead.

The chase was on, the local Reverend Mr E. T. Champnes who had initially responded to Sarah Harts cry of help, ran to the railway station to catch up with Tawell but unfortunately he arrived there just too late, he saw him board the 7.42pm service to Paddington.

The quick thinking Reverend immediately consulted with the station master who then arranged for an electric telegraph to be sent to Paddington Railway Station the message read, *'a murder has just been committed at Salt Hill and the suspected murderer was seen to take a first class ticket to London that left Slough at 7.42pm, he is in the garb of a Kwaker (sic) with a brown great coat on which reaches his feet. He is in the last compartment of the second first class carriage'*

The Railway Police

The electric telegraph did not have a letter 'Q' hence the spelling of Quaker.

At Paddington Railway Station a clerk ran the message to the Great Western Railway Police Office where it was passed to the Duty Sergeant, Sgt William Williams, he put on a plain long overcoat over his police uniform and waited and met the train as it arrived.

Sgt Williams then followed Tawell out of the station and onto an omnibus and the Sgt sat in the conductors chair, Tawell alighted at Princes Street and obviously thinking the Sgt was the conductor he gave him the correct fare of 6p and he got off the omnibus followed by Sgt Williams, he then proceeded to follow him along the dimly lit streets of London, firstly to a sweet shop then to a local coffee house, the Sgt kept him under observation until he went into a lodging house in Scotts Yard.

Being satisfied that was where Tawell was legitimately living he returned to Paddington where he visited a colleague and friend, Police Inspector Wiggins of the Metropolitan Police. The following morning having confirmed all the details of the murder of Sarah Hart with colleagues from Slough, the two officers went off in search of Tawell.

The first disappointment was he was not at the lodgings, but they found him in the coffee house, the same coffee house as Sgt Williams had visited yesterday. John Tawell was arrested by the two officers and taken into custody and he protested by saying that he was not in Slough yesterday, the Sgt said, 'You was, sir and you got out of the train onto an omnibus and then gave me six pence for the fare' it mattered not he was taken away and later charged that day with the murder of Miss Sarah Hart by poisoning.

The trial opened at Aylesbury County Court on 12th March 1845 with Tawell charged with murder by poisoning by use of prussic acid, the trial lasted for two days and within half an hour of the jury retiring to consider their verdict they returned and had found him guilty of murder.

The Judge donned the black cap and John Tawell was sentenced to death by hanging.

On 28th March 1845 John Tawell was publicly hanged to death on gallows erected outside the court and over 10,000 people attended to view the public hanging.

A railway policeman, Sergeant William Williams had become the first policeman to arrest someone for murder following the use of the electric telegraph.

CHAPTER SEVEN

GREAT GOLD ROBBERY (THE PLAN)

As with the increase in railway traffic naturally came with it the increase in crime, we know by 1838 that trains are carrying Her Majesty's mail and in 1855 we had the first of two very famous robberies committed on the rail network, the first of these is what is affectingly known as 'The Great Gold Robbery'

On the night of 15th May 1855, three London firms each handed to Chaplin and Co, Carriers, a box of gold for conveyance from London, via Folkestone and Boulogne, for Paris each box was weighed and sealed at the carriers office and taken to London Bridge Station to be put onto the South Eastern Railway, at the railway station the boxes were placed into iron travelling safes and double locked with two Chubb patent locks, the keys to the safes were entrusted with the railway staff from London to Folkestone, then with the Captain of the cross channel steamer the 'Lord Warden.'

When the 'Lord Warden' reached Boulogne the boxes were taken from the safes and weighed, none of the boxes showed signs of interference but one weighed 40 pounds less than the other two, nevertheless they were transferred locked to their final destination in Paris.

On arrival at Paris the safes were unlocked and the boxes were found to contain lead shot, a total of 200lb of gold bars to the value of £12,000 and a quantity of American 10 dollar coins were missing. In present day values it would be estimated that the load would be valued at one million pounds.

Enquiries were made and it soon became obvious that the investigators believed that the swop of gold to lead shot took place aboard the train on its journey from London Bridge to Folkestone.

After many months of enquiries by both English and French Police, including the South Eastern Railway Police they found nothing, several dozen people were interviewed, some were even arrested but still it came to nothing, but the suspicious still lay with the railway staff at Folkestone.

The South Easter Railway even offered a reward but still nothing was forthcoming.

In August 1855 Edward Agar who was a career criminal was arrested for passing a false cheque and sentenced to transportation to Australia for life. Before his arrest Agar had been associating with a young woman called Fanny Kay who shared a child with him, whilst awaiting transportation Agar often thought about and wrote to Miss Kay and he had made a provision for her with a William Pierce an ex-railway worker who had been dismissed in 1850, Agar had allegedly given Pierce £7,000 to pass on to Miss Kay but she had not received a penny and by 1856 she was destitute.

This caused a vicious quarrel with Pierce and she decided to go to see the governor of Newgate Prison where Agar was currently being held and she told him an interesting story, the governor contacted a Mr Rees who was investigating the theft of the gold for the Railway company and Miss Kay was taken to London Bridge to see Mr Rees.

Miss Kay then made a full statement to Mr Rees and soon he was on his way to see Agar who by now was in the prison hulk at Portland on his final leg before transportation to Australia.

When it was explained by Mr Rees what Pierce had done then Agar decided that the only way he could pay

Pierce back was to tell the truth and to tell Mr Rees what had happened, in due course Agar made a full written statement describing how the gold had been stolen and by whom.

In the first instance Mr Rees decided that in the investigation he wanted two Metropolitan Police Officers, Inspector Williamson and Inspector Thornton to assist him, and after Miss Kay made her detailed witness statement it was decided that she would live at the home address of Inspector Thornton at the expense of South Eastern Railway.

It was felt that she was too valuable of a witness to be expected to live anywhere else.

CHAPTER EIGHT

GREAT GOLD ROBBERY (THE EXECUTION)

The story of the theft of the gold gradually unfolded, Agar had met Pierce many years earlier when Pierce worked as a ticket printer for South Eastern Railway, and when Agar returned from America after spending some time there he met Pierce again, and they discussed the possibility of stealing some gold that was frequently shipped from London to Paris on the South Eastern Railway network.

Initially Agar thought that the task would be impossible unless they could take or get impressions of the keys cut and Agar obviously wanted to know how many other people would know about this obviously the less who knew the better.

Pierce said two would know, one was Burgess the railway guard and the other was Tester at that time a station master. Agar agreed to have a closer look at the plan and in May 1854, Agar and Pierce went to Folkestone for two weeks where they spent the time looking at the workings of the trains, but they soon bought suspicions on themselves and were noticed by Inspector Hazell and some other police officers from the South Eastern Railway Police.

Pierce returned to London but Agar remained in Folkestone and with the assistance of Tester began to make friends with some of the railway staff at Folkestone, in particular he visited public houses and cafes frequented by the railway staff and was concentrating particular on one man who handled the keys of the travelling safes in the course of his normal duties.

Inspector Hazell thinking Agar was in fact a pickpocket warned this particular railway clerk about Agars close attention and Agar suspecting something was wrong quickly left Folkestone for London.

By this time Burgess had been introduced into the circle, so the four of them Agar, Pierce, Tester and Burgess regularly began to meet to discuss plans. Their favourite meeting place would be the Green Man public house or the White Hart public house both close to London Bridge.

The Railway Police

It seemed Tester was regarded as an able man by his superiors and while the conspirators were still discussing the ways and means of how to carry out the crime, fate played very nicely into their hands, Tester was promoted and transferred to London and found himself in the very same office that dealt with the security of valuable goods and also he was responsible for the rota of the guards, what good be better for the budding thieves.

During July the safe locks were being returned to Chubb for alteration and Tester in his new role would briefly have the new keys in his possession, the new safe had two locks with two different keys, Chubb at first only sending one key to each safe, Tester on receipt of the keys then briefly handed them to Agar who made an impression of the keys from wax.

The difficulty now was to get an impression of the second key because there were two locks on each safe, so arrangements were in hand and Agar arranged to have a box of bullion sent on a train to Folkestone where he would collect it using the assumed name, Agar went to Folkestone to collect the bullion and watched as the railway booking clerk simply took a key from a cupboard in the office to open the safe with and to remove the bullion.

He was joined in Folkestone by Pierce and when the opportunity arose in the absence of the booking clerk from the office, Pierce walked into the office took the key gave it to Agar who took a wax impression of the key they then returned the key and walked off it was all over in seconds, but what they had now was the two impressions needed so that they could now have keys made to open the safes.

To make certain, Agar travelled several times to Folkestone in the guards van with Burgess and continually adjusted the keys in the safe locks until they fitted perfectly. At this stage they decided having gone to so much trouble and care that they would not attempt the robbery until a large amount of gold was passing, they aimed for a quantity in value of £12,000, which they estimated would weigh about two hundred pounds.

Agar then went with Pierce to the Shot Tower on Hungerford Bridge where they bought two hundred pound weight of lead shot, and over the next few months moved the lead shot by placing it into specially made leather courier bags and the rest in carpet bags and night after night they moved into to London Bridge Station using different routes to get there. They now waited for a prearranged signal from Burgess as to when a likely load of bullion was expected.

On the night of 15th May 1855 both Burgess and Tester tipped Agar and Pierce off, they both then bought two first class tickets to Dover and they handed the carpet bags to a porter to place in the guards van, they also took with them two half tickets to Ostend. Pierce took a seat in a compartment and Agar went un-observed into Burgess's van.

The three boxes of bullion were loaded onto the South Eastern train and off it went, shortly after Agar who was also armed with a mallet and chisel and other tools and wax and tapers he needed once it came to resealing the boxes.

He opened the first safe with the keys that he had made and knocked off the iron clamps from the box, he opened the box and took out the gold bars substituting them for the lead shot, re-replaced the iron fastenings and nails and resealed the boxes with the wax and tapers. Agar had completed the first box and when they reached Redhill, Tester was waiting for him and Agar gave him a gold bar.

Pierce then joined Agar in the van to help with the other two boxes they opened them both successfully but found that they had not bought enough lead shot with them and this of course accounted for the discrepancy when the three safes reached Boulogne.

Before they left the van Pierce and Agar cleared up all their mess and swept the van out and everything was left perfectly normal. On arrival at Folkestone the safes were taken from the train in the normal manner to be placed on the cross channel steamer and onto Paris where the theft was discovered.

Agar and Pierce continued on the train to Dover with the gold bars which were now safely contained in the original carpet bags in Burgess's van on the train. On reaching Dover they got off took the carpet bags with them and Agar threw the mallet and chisel into the sea.

Both men then returned to London with their load of gold bars which was safely hidden in carpet bags and took them to Agars house in Shephard's Bush. A furnace was built and day after day they melted the gold bars down and sold them on to various individuals and the proceeds of the sale were shared out between them.

In the end share out, Burgess received £700.00 (worth about £50,000 today) and the rest including Agar £600.00 each (worth about £41,000 today).

CHAPTER NINE

GREAT GOLD ROBBERY (THE ARRESTS)

In November 1856 William Pierce and James Burgess were arrested in London and shortly afterwards William Tester was arrested in Deal, Kent.

The trial of the three men opened at the Old Bailey in London on 10th January 1857 and the two most important witnesses against them was Miss Fanny Kay and Mr Edward Agar. At the trial the defence made the most of the fact that the prosecution relied on and in the main evidence from an accomplice, but once the modus operandi of the robbery was known, the investigating officers with the assistance of the South Eastern Railway Police were able to build up other evidence that eventually connected the three men to the robbery.

A search of Agars house revealed small amounts of gold which of course corroborated what he had told the police.

The trial lasted three days and the jury deliberated for a total of ten minutes, Burgess and Tester were sentenced to transportation for fourteen years and Pierce was convicted of simple larceny in other words simple theft and was sentenced to two years imprisonment with the first, 12th and 24th month to be spent in solitary confinement.

It is interesting to note that the Judge decided that a railway carriage could not be regarded as a dwelling house of the railway company, so the original counts of larceny in a dwelling house were dismissed.

It was however a remarkable case the crime had all the hall marks of a great robbery, it had the audacity, the link with the man with the inside information, the planning, the reconnaissance, the patience, perhaps even the greed that eventually bought the men down.

It of course remained the biggest bank robbery on the railway until almost a hundred years later when in 1963 when the railway suffered what has become known as 'The Great Train Robbery'

CHAPTER TEN

THE FIRST MURDER

The first murder on board a train took place on Saturday 9th July 1864; it began when the 9.50pm train from Fenchurch Street Railway Station on the North London Railway line arrived at Hackney Railway Station at about 11 minutes past ten.

Two bank clerks boarded the train and went to an empty first class carriage and sat down, and one of the clerks almost immediately found fresh blood on his hand, they both immediately alighted the train and called over a railway guard who made a more detailed examination of the carriage and he found blood all over some cushions and on a door he also found a black beaver hat, a stick and a bag.

The guard locked the door and contacted the station master at Chalk Farm Railway Station by electric telegraph, and on the arrival of the station master it was decided to detach the carriage from the rest of the train and send it to Bow Railway Station for further investigation. The hat and other property were handed to the Metropolitan Police.

At 10.20pm the same night a driver travelling in the opposite direction saw something on the floor just outside Bow Railway Station, he stopped his train and found a badly beaten man lying there, with the assistance of others the man was taken to a nearby public house to raise help, but he sadly died of his injuries. However he was subsequently identified as seventy year old Thomas Briggs, a chief clerk at the Lombard Bank in the City of London.

The bag and stick that had been found in the carriage confirmed the identity of the deceased, and that it would appear that robbery was clearly the motive as the victims gold watch and chain was missing along with his gold eye glasses.

The first important information came from a jeweller named curiously John Death, he owned a jewellers shop in Cheapside and he gave a description of a man he believed to be German, who had called at his shop on 11th July 1864 and exchanged a gold chain, the gold chain was later positively identified as belonging to the victim Mr Briggs.

The Railway Police

Next on 18th July 1864, a cabman told police that he had in his house a small cardboard box bearing the name of Death, which had been given to one of his children by a young German named Franz Muller, Muller had previously been engaged to the cab man's eldest daughter.

Enquiries now showed that Muller had sailed for New York on 15th July 1864 in the sailing ship 'Victoria' the cab man also stated that the black beaver hat found in the train, was purchased by him for Mr Muller he also gave police a picture of Muller that was also positively identified by the jeweller Mr Death.

So the police enquiries were going well they had more than enough information to believe that the murderer of Mr Briggs was Franz Muller.

The mechanism for the detection so far had worked well and a warrant for the arrest of Franz Muller was granted at Bow Street Magistrates Court and on 19th July 1864, Police Inspector Tanner and Police Sergeant Clarke left Euston Railway Station to travel to Liverpool, on 20th July 1864 they sailed for New York on the steamship 'City of Manchester' and arrived on 5th August 1864, three full weeks before Muller arrived, and when he did eventually arrive in New York he was arrested and when searched, found in his possession was the victims gold watch and hat.

Extradition proceedings took place between 26th August and 3rd September 1864 which was successful and the two police officers then left New York with their prisoner Muller. A large crowd of people awaited them at Euston Railway Station when they eventually arrived all wanted to take a look at the man who was accused of the first ever murder on a train.

The trial of Frank Muller took place on 27th October 1864 at the Old Bailey and he was found guilty of the murder of Mr Briggs and was sentenced to death. Muller confessed to the crime immediately before being publically executed by hanging.

The public hanging of Muller took place amid scene of drunkenness and disorder and was to be one of the last public executions.

It was also the first murder on a railway and the pursuit across the Atlantic raised the imagination of the public.

The murder of Mr Briggs bought about the fitting of compulsory communication between the passengers and the train driver; the communication cord had arrived and with it came the view that if Mr Briggs could have pulled the communication cord quite possibly he may have been alive today.

CHAPTER ELEVEN

THE DECLINE OF THE RAILWAY POLICE

As every piece of track was laid, as ever railway station opened and as every railway company which covered England, Wales and Scotland was formed it had to be policed by the railway police.

I mean we do know that some of the railway companies particularly the London and North Western Railway and the Great Western Railway had by now formed their own Criminal Investigation Department by 1863, but most of the other railway companies for ease seemed to call on the expertise of the Metropolitan Police and their experienced detectives if and when they needed it.

But the problem with the railway police is that they were expected to be jack of all trades and master of none, they were expected to be ticket officers, guards, porters, and do other non-police roles and then in the next breath they were policeman protecting property, protecting people, investigating crime and arresting the offenders on the railway as and when the need arose.

There appeared to be very little discipline amongst the various railway companies, the training was poor and if anything at all it seemed at this time the general view was that the railway police were in decline, particularly at a time when the 1856 County Police Act came into being and which allowed county police forces to be formed and they were much better organised and far more professional, the railway police appeared to being left behind somewhat but of course not all of them.

The London North Western Railway, The Midland and the North East Railway still maintained a fairly large and professional police force on its railways, they were in full uniform with police powers, whereas other railway companies reduced the size of their forces, their duties being restricted to those in the company's best interest in other words it was most surely down to cost.

The Railway Police

Often they had to perform non police duties and related tasks and one railway who I will not name employed railway men unfit for normal railway duties as constables on their railway in other words anybody will do and as cheap as you can get.

A lot of the railways seemed to rely heavily on the new county police forces to do the 'real' work and they hired in detectives when they needed them and one of the most strangest stories to come out of this was that the London, Brighton and South Coast Railway had their own police force on the railway with a uniform but they had no police powers so what purpose did they serve.

The railway police at the turn of the century was therefore a hotchpotch of various forces, which was covering various railway companies some with efficient, disciplined and organised uniformed men others with old, idle and undisciplined officers, police in name only and with a variety of duties to perform.

In Ilford one poor railway police sergeant was blamed for a minor collision on the track because he was dealing with a disturbance involving passengers at the station, when he should have changed the points on the railway track.

And in the world of the railway things were not standing still on 10th January 1863, the first section of the London Underground was opened between Paddington Railway Station and Farringdon Railway Station via Kings Cross

Railway Station, and it was to be called the Metropolitan Railway or as it is known today the Metropolitan Line and within a few weeks of opening it was carrying 26,000 passengers a day.

This of course was something new for the railway police and they were expected to police it.

CHAPTER TWELVE

PERCY MAPLETON LEFROY

On the afternoon of Monday 27th June 1881 the 2.00pm train from London Bridge Railway Station arrived at Preston Park Railway Station in Brighton, a ticket collector observed a man step out of the first class carriage he appeared badly injured and covered in blood and was in a distressed state.

The ticket collector went to the man's aid and he informed the ticket collector he had just been attacked on the train, and he went on to describe the two men who had attacked him. He said he remembered nothing else until the train had reached Brighton.

The condition of this somewhat strange and battered passenger who gave his name as Percy Mapleton Lefroy, alerted the station master and so he decided to take the man to the local police station at Brighton Town Hall while the ticket collector went off to inform the railway police.

Lefroy made an official complaint of assault and was taken to the local hospital to be treated. He then went back to the police station where he was interviewed by several police officers including would you believe the Chief Constable of the Brighton Police.

In the meantime the carriage where Lefroy had stepped from was moved into the sidings and searched, the police found three bullet marks and there was blood everywhere, on the footboards, on the mat, on a door and on a newspaper and hanker-chief that had been left in the carriage. They appeared to have been a fierce and violent struggle that had taken place inside the carriage.

In spite of the really suspicious incident and findings in the carriage and the strange reaction of Lefroy, neither the Brighton Police or the Railway Police decided to detain him for further investigation of his claim and of course on what they had found in the carriage.

So he was allowed to travel on to London but he was to be escorted on the journey by a DS George Holmes. During this period some of the railway companies including the London, Brighton and South Coast Railway supplemented their own staff by the employment of Metropolitan Police officers, who were seconded by New Scotland Yard for this purpose, the salaries of the officers were paid by the railway company to the Metropolitan Police. DS Holmes was one of those officers.

However the end result of this particular case and the widespread criticism of his negligence surrounding it caused New Scotland Yard to publically disown the officer.

When Lefroy and DS Holmes were travelling back to London, a search of the railway line was organised and led by the railway police and in the Balcombe railway tunnel, railway police and staff found a body, he was of an elderly man and he had been shot and stabbed and near to his body was a knife smeared in blood, the elderly gent was identified as a man called Mr Gold who came from Brighton. It was also learned that he had been robbed of his watch and chain and some money.

The news of the finding of the dead body was passed along the railway line and at Three Bridges Railway Station, the station master informed the officer DS Holmes what had happened and the officer was instructed by the police at Brighton not to let Lefroy out of his sight for any reason whatsoever.

However Lefroy talked the officer into taking him to a relative's house in Surrey later that night apparently to get a change of clothes, they arrived at 9.30pm, Lefroy went inside and the officer for some unknown reason remained outside the house, he stood there for quite a while and when he made enquiries at the house it was discovered that Lefroy had gone out of the back of the building and disappeared without the officer noticing.

A countrywide search was made to find Lefroy and a conference was held at Brighton Railway Station, where the entire railway staff involved was questioned by senior detectives.

The inquest for Mr Gold was opened on 29th June 1881 and DS Holmes in particular and the other railway police involved were given a tough time by the coroner in the witness box and quite rightly so, at the conclusion of the inquest the coroner returned a verdict of wilful murder against Lefroy.

The railway company offered a large reward for the arrest of Lefroy as they felt it was their fault that he had got away. Lefroy was eventually arrested nearly two weeks later on 8th July 1881 in a lodging house in Stepney, London and blood stained clothes were recovered from his room.

Lefroy was later charged with the murder of Mr Gold and in due course was tried at Maidstone Assizes and the court heard from several witnesses including DS Holmes, and a number of railway staff.

He was found guilty of murder by the jury in less than ten minutes; Lefroy whose real name was Mapleton was hanged at Lewes Prison on 19th November 1881.

The London, Brighton and South Coast Railway were subjected to a great deal of ridicule and no doubt many police officers were urged to have greater care in the future but they did not have to worry too much because it was another 16 years before there was another murder on the railway.

CHAPTER THIRTEEN
THE UNSOLVED MURDER

The next murder on the railway was on 11th February 1897 when Mr Edward Berry was waiting on the platform at Waterloo Railway Station for the arrival of the 7.42pm train from Hounslow. He was awaiting the arrival of his fiancée Elizabeth Annie Camp, at 8.25pm the train arrived but although most of the passengers got off there was no sign of his girlfriend, obviously Mr Berry quickly began to panic.

There was further down the platform, he could see some sort of a commotion and he could see various railway officials and the railway police running to the scene of where the crowd was now gathering.

A body had been found in the carriage of the train and it was his girlfriend, Miss Camp, it would appear that she had been beaten to death by someone and then the body was pushed under the seats in the carriage on the train.

The body was removed from the carriage and taken to St Thomas's hospital where Mr Berry identified the body as that of Elizabeth Annie Camp his girlfriend; the cause of death unfortunately was very obvious as the head of the woman was badly beaten up. There was no sign of a sexual motive but it was noticed that the pockets of her coat had been rifled and apparently emptied so therefore robbery must have been the motive.

Detective Superintendent Robinson of the London, South Western Railway Police with the assistance of Chief Inspector Marshall of Scotland Yard took up the murder investigation.

A search of the carriage revealed very little, except for a broken umbrella, a set of cufflinks and that was all that they ever found, and throughout the murder enquiry a green purse belonging to the victim was never found despite several searches. The railway line and embankment from Hounslow to Waterloo was searched several times as best as the railway police could do and they did find a chemists pestle that had blood and hairs on which was subsequently identified as the murder weapon.

The inquest into the death was opened in Lambeth on 17th February 1897 and from there after the inquest was adjourned weekly in the anticipation that the railway police along with Scotland Yard would find the murderer of Miss Camp.

But despite interviewing several suspects the killer was never found, they even had one man surrender himself saying that he had committed the murder, he however was found to be a mental defective.

On 7th April 1897 the inquest was finally held into the death of Miss Camp and the jury returned a verdict of 'wilful murder against some person or persons unknown'

We know that Detective Superintendent Robinson had his suspicions about who may have committed the murder but he could not connect any of the suspects with the murder weapon or the train and the murder of poor Miss Camp was never solved.

CHAPTER FOURTEEN
REORGANISATION OF THE RAILWAY POLICE

The turn of the century was a time for change with the railway police and it had to, from 1900 several of the railway companies reorganised their own police forces. In particular The London, Brighton and South Coast Railway virtually reformed their police force from scratch and they were followed by the Great Eastern Railway, the North Eastern and Midland Railway, the Caledonian Railway and the Great Western Railway.

Reorganisation was to pull the railway police into the 20th century with a sharp tug and it was certainly needed and indeed it would make them more professional, pay conditions and uniforms were improved and upgraded and the establishment of the railway police increased almost everywhere.

One railway even provided training for its constables and facilities to improve their education, training and manual of guidance's were issued to all constables, so at least all the railway police were heading in the right direction, it was a massive attempt to form a fully trained professional police force to police the railway.

These reforms and better training came at the right time for the railways because the Great War was to begin in 1914 and it put a massive amount of pressure onto the railway infrastructure and of course on its railway police.

There were numerous attacks by the enemy on the railway infrastructure and several railway stations were damaged by enemy bombings and the railway also suffered many casualties during the four years of the war.

In some railway police forces more than half of the men were conscripted into the role and others were supplemented by special constables but at least under the reorganisation they were all getting much the same type of training and much the same rates of pay.

In 1914 the Great Eastern Railway Police recruited nine women as special constables, one of the first if not the first railway company to do so.

Also at the turn of the century the railway network suffered two deliberate attacks on the railway infrastructure and its staff and passengers, on 26th April 1897 a bomb was left by an unidentified anarchist group on a Metropolitan train and it exploded when the train reached Aldersgate Street Railway Station, there one was fatality, a Harry Pitts aged 36 years, although 60 were injured, 10 of those serious, the bombers were never found despite both the railway police and New Scotland Yard conducting a vigorous investigation.

In February 1913 a bomb was discovered at Westbourne Park Railway Station possibly planted by 'the suffragettes' who were very active at the time, fortunately the bomb failed to explode and there were no injuries and no damage but once again the bombers were never found.

But of course the bombings or attempted bombings were all new to the railway police and something else that they had to deal with and something they were not use to and were not trained to deal with but you very quickly learnt.

Of course in later years as I will discuss later in the book, the railway network became a popular target for the Provisional Irish Republican Army (PIRA) both in 1939 at the start of the Second World War, and more particularly in the 1970's and the 1990s.

And more recently although nothing to do with PIRA we had the terrorist bomb attacks of 7th July 2005 on the London Transport system.

In 1917 the first policewomen were sworn in on the North Eastern Railway, there was already women railway police on the Great Eastern and Great Western Railways but these were the first for the North Eastern Railway.

But there were still more changes to come after the end of the First World War many of the military personnel returned to their pre-war employment with the British Railway Police, and in 1919 the pay of the railway police was standardised throughout and the Railway Police Federation was formed.

This was to look after the wellbeing of the railway police and of course it was something that had been badly needed for many a year.

Perhaps the biggest shake up of the railway police to date came with the 1921 Railways Act, and what that did was to amalgamate all the railway systems throughout the country and there was over one hundred of them, probably as many as twenty of them had their own police forces and they were all to be amalgamated into four main and purposeful groups.

The Great Western Railway (GWR) The London and North Eastern Railway (LNR) The London, Midland and Scotland Railway (LMS) and The Southern Railway (SR).

Each had its own police force led by a Chief of Police, the four forces were organised in the same way, each split into a number of divisions led by a Superintendent and in turn divided into a number of divisional posts led by an Inspector.

The reorganisation of the railway police was moving very quickly but it was to make them more professional in everything they did it was what they needed and wanted.

Detectives worked with their uniformed colleagues at most locations although many non-police roles were retained by the railway police such as officers acting as railway crossing keepers or unlocking, locking and the sealing of railway wagons.

CHAPTER FIFTEEN

THE INTRODUCTION OF POLICE DOGS

Policemen and police dogs have always gone together like bread and butter, and the first dogs used by police can be traced way back to the 15th century, when the then parish constables took dogs with them when they went out on night patrol. It has been suggested that these dogs were probably the pets of the parish constables, and they are likely to have taken the dogs with them for company during the long and often quite night, rather than as any sort of deterrent but that is apparently where it all started.

The very first experiment with dogs that we do know about took place in 1888, when the then Commissioner of the Metropolitan Police, Mr Charles Warren tested the effectiveness of two bloodhounds with a view to using them in the search for the infamous Victorian killer 'Jack the Ripper' however the experiment was a total disaster, after one of the dogs bit the commissioner and then both dogs ran off, it took a police search to find the dogs again so that was the end of police dogs for the time being.

Police dogs were being used by the police on the continent with apparent more success, and in 1906 Colonel Richardson an ardent dog trainer tried to get the Metropolitan Police to start a dog section but they were very reluctant, but they did send representatives later that year to France to see the working of the police dog.

But they came back very unimpressed and when they submitted their report to the commissioner they stated 'the dogs appear useful but we feel that London is no place for a police dog.'

In November 1907 Superintendent Dobie, of the North Eastern Railway Police, the police force responsible for the policing of the docks at Hull, together with a Mr Geedes, Chief Goods Manager of Hull Docks, and three other railway policemen went to Ghent, in Belgium and observed the police dogs in use over there. All the men were suitable impressed with the workings of the dogs and on their return the Superintendent asked Inspector Dobson to set something similar up at the docks.

Inspector Dobson decided to use Airedale Terriers, not the usual Alsatian dog as he believed them to have a better sense of smell and their wiry coat was less likely to pick up mud from the docks and for that reason they would need less grooming.

The very first police dogs went out on patrol with their handlers at Hull Docks in 1908, and initially there were four dogs. The local press picked up on it and one reported, 'In a novel way by the North Eastern Railway Police are going to use dogs as detectives on the docks.' The dogs were very simply trained, they were trained to obey the police whistle and they were trained to chase and stop people running away from the policeman it was as easy as that.

In November 1908 the scheme was extended to Hartlepool Docks and then onto the Tyne Docks, then onto the Middlesbrough Docks, all of course policed by the North Eastern Railway and Superintendent Dobie.

The dogs were only used at night and were probably not specific to an individual handler, and they were trained by the use of treats and their role was to protect the man in the police uniform, indeed attack anyone who is not in a police uniform and if not in a uniform at night walking around the docks then you can bet he was up to no good.

So the dog was trained to attack him, it was said that they would even attack the police dog handlers if they were not wearing their uniform.

There is a story from the 1910 edition of the North Eastern railway magazine, which tells us that one morning a railway policeman and his dog was patrolling St Andrews Dock in Hull when they observed a man loitering in a suspicious manner, the policeman called on him to stop and the man took no notice so the officer slipped the dog off its leash, it apparently chased, caught and very soon bought the man down to the floor begging for mercy.

Having arrested the man the police officer made a detailed search around and found a window to the refreshment room broken, he entered the room and called upon those inside to come out otherwise he would take the muzzle of his dog and send the dog in, a voice said, 'put the muzzle back sir, we will come out' and out stepped two rather burly and obviously afraid of dogs burglars.

The policeman with his dog then marched the three of them back to the police station, allegedly one of the first arrests by use of a police dog; well surely the magazine would not lie would it.

After the Great War of 1914-1918 had finished the dog section of the railway police was made subject of a review, and in 1923 the Hull Dock Police now decided to use

Alsatians as it was the favoured dog of the German army during the war.

It took until the late 1920's for other 'non-railway' police to become interested in the use of dogs and 1938 before it became the norm for all the police to have a dog section with their force.

CHAPTER SIXTEEN

THE RAILWAY POLICE AND THEIR DOGS

Dogs continued to play a big part in railway policing and after the end of the Second World War in 1945, and the setting up of the British Transport Commission in 1949 there was a total of 75 police dogs being used by the railway police.

During the 1960's there was a purpose built police dog training centre constructed in Hertfordshire, and now police dogs and their handlers were being based at many railway stations and docks throughout the country including Southampton Docks who had their first police dogs in 1962.

It was in Southampton in 1973 where the first dog was trained to detect cannabis, as the drug was regularly being illegally imported into this country by use of the railway system. Between 1973 and 1974 arrests by police dogs and their handlers rose to 908 people which is over 2 a day no mean feat.

In 1980 Police Constable Parkinson of the railway police now known as the British Transport Police (BTP), was the first officer with his dog to undergo training for detecting explosives, in 1982 we had the first female dog handler in the force.

Probably the most dramatic story involving railway police and their dogs was on 21st December 1988, a terrorist bomb exploded aboard Pan—Am Flight 103 flying from London Heathrow to New York's John F Kennedy airport, the aeroplane crashed onto the Scottish town of Lockerbie and a total of 270 people including 11 from the town of Lockerbie were killed.

Two dog handlers from the British Transport Police with their dogs arrived at the scene and began a tour of duty that was to last for 33 hours, the officers and their dogs found 23 bodies. They were later joined by two other dog handlers and they remained on site for a total of four weeks. The involvement of these four police officers and their police dogs were such that when the trial took place of two men believed involved in the bombing some 11 years in Holland, all four officers had to attend to give evidence relating to the incident and the recovery of the bodies.

So now police dogs are very much a part of the railways and I suppose we may have to thank Superintendent Dobie way back in 1907 for the introduction of dogs with the railway police.

CHAPTER SEVENTEEN

RAIL CRASHES

I would imagine that rail crashes involving rolling stock which results in death and injury are perhaps one of the worst types of incidents that the railway police have to deal with, and we must remember as long as there are trains, railways and people there will always be accidents.

Since the first ever known recorded accident involving rolling stock was way back in 1815, when there was a boiler explosion on board the 'Bruntons Mechanical Traveller' which was a very early steam locomotive whilst it was stationary on a plate way at Philadelphia, County Durham, and a total of 16 persons mainly sightseers were killed.

Since then there has been over 180 rail accidents involving rolling stock and I am in no doubt that the railway police would almost certainly be one of the first people on the scene of some of these horrific accidents where people have been killed or seriously injured.

I know there is nothing at all amusing in accidents but on a lighter note in April 1831 at Newton Junction on the Liverpool-Manchester line, PC Bates of the Liverpool and Manchester Railway Police caused an accident when he failed to change a set of points when asleep at his post, he was fined £3 by the local magistrates, see we are all human.

At Bagworth in Leicestershire May 1833, a train collided with a farmers cart on a level crossing and as a result of that accident the locomotive whistle was invented so in the future all trains sounded a loud whistle when they came to a level crossing.

In December 1879 what is known now as the Tay Bridge disaster occurred, a total of 75 persons died when a bridge that the train was travelling over collapsed during a severe weather.

Another horrific accident was the Armagh disaster when in June 1889 a total of 80 persons were killed and over 170 injured when some runaway carriages hit a train, this is by far Irelands worst train crash.

And on they went sometimes two or three a year, really serious train accidents involving rolling stock, some caused by accident others perhaps by sheer neglect and others by people thinking 'it won't happen to me.'

From the day the first train ran until today over 1000 persons have died as a result of train accidents, and every one of those accidents have to be investigated and in most cases this would be down to the railway police and the detectives of the railway police and of course with assistance from other forces as well.

In February 2001 we had what is known as the 'Selby rail crash' this was a high speed train crash near to the village of Selby, North Yorkshire.

It occurred at 6.13am when a Land Rover Defender towing a loaded trailer which was carrying a Renault motor vehicle swerved off the M62 motorway and onto the East Coast main line, the vehicle went down an embankment and onto the southbound track, the driver of the vehicle a Mr Gary Hart began to use his mobile phone to alert the emergency services, almost immediately the Land Rover was then struck by a southbound GNER intercity train heading from Newcastle to London.

As a result of the collision the train was deflected onto another track and into the path of a freight train, immediately before the double collision the Intercity was travelling at 88mph and the freight train was travelling at

54mph with an estimated closing speed of 142mph, the collision between the trains was the highest speed railway incident that has occurred in the United Kingdom.

The result of the collision was horrific with a total of ten people dead including both train drivers and over 82 injured some very seriously. A full investigation was mounted by officers from the North Yorkshire Police with assistance from the local railway police.

In due course on 13th December 2001 the driver of the Land Rover, Mr Gary Hart was charged with 10 counts of causing death by dangerous driving and was sentenced to five years imprisonment.

However the most deadly rail crash ever in the UK happened at 6.20am on 22nd May 1915, in Scotland near Gretna Green at Quintinshill an intermediate signal box which had four lines, the two main lines were known as the up line and the down line, and two passing loop sidings again one on the up side and one on the down side.

What happened next is quite horrific, the two passing loop sidings already had trains in them; there was a stationary goods train on the down loop and a stationary train of empty coal trucks on the up loop.

The signal man then shunted a local train onto the up line to allow two express trains to pass the signal box at speed on the down line.

The same signal man forgot about the local train and allowed a special troop train to use the up line and it resulted in a collision between the local train and the troop train, then almost immediately the second of the express trains ran into the collision, and because three trains were in a collision the impact deflected the trains onto both the up and down loop sidings, so in the space of minutes five trains were involved in a collision.

The impact of the crash was devastating in total 226 died and a further 246 were injured. It is the worst train crash for fatalities in the United Kingdom.

The majority of the dead and injured were territorial soldiers of the 7th Battalion of the Royal Scots based in Edinburgh. A roll call of the soldiers made at 4.00pm later that day revealed only 57 were present out of 500 who were on the train.

Also what made the crash more severe was a fire as the troop train had carriages made of wood, there was of course gas lights because it was early morning and dark, there was coal from the bunkers of the steam trains and it is possible more people died as the result of the fire than the rail crash.

It was also the first major British disaster in which a great number of the dead were never recovered as bodies being wholly consumed by the fire. Another contributory factor was that it took the fire appliances four hours to get to the scene of the crash because of the remoteness of the signal box.

The rescuers even found the bodies of three young children who to date have never been identified.

And who was to blame for the accident? Well two signal men George Meakin and James Tinsley were sentenced to terms of imprisonment for culpable homicide due to neglect of their duties. Basically it was said that if both signal men had obeyed the operating rules and used the safety devices provided then the accident would not have occurred.

In other words because these men were sloppy and neglectful in their duty a total of 226 people died and over 246 were injured.

We do know that the railway police at the time would have been actively involved in the above rail accident and subsequent investigations that followed and of course the prosecution of the two signal men.

CHAPTER EIGHTEEN
THE GENERAL STRIKE OF 1926

In 1926 we had the General Strike which lasted for ten days from 3rd May 1926 until 13th May 1926.

It was called by the General Council of the Trades Union Congress better known as the TUC, it was and turned out to be an unsuccessful attempt to force the British Government of the day to act to prevent wage reduction and worsening conditions for coal miners in the British coal mines.

Essentially it was caused by the First World War, Britain was exporting less coal because of the war so of course there was less demand for it, and after the end on the war and in the period between 1920 and 1924 other countries in particular the United States, Poland and Germany were benefitting from their particular strong coal fields.

In 1925 the Dawes Plan was initiated by the government of the day and this led to Germany making and exporting 'free coal' to countries like France and Italy as part of their repatriation after the First World War.

This led to the owners of the British mines still wanting to maximise and normalise profits, so this led to the coal miners being expected to work longer hours for the same pay in other words a form of wage reduction, so the coal industry was thrown into disarray.

This led to the support for the coal miners from all sides of industry in Britain in the form of the General Strike.

On the first day of the strike, the coal miners walked out closely followed by workers from the road, rail, bus, docks, printing, steel, iron, building, gas and electricity companies as they all went on strike.

This of course led to many volunteers particularly from middle class people who were against the strike, to begin to work in some of the striking industries and on the railway in particular, to keep it moving and to assist and to know who was who, the railway police issued the volunteers with special identity cards.

The government recruited over 226,000 special constables to assist with the disorder on the streets, and once again the railway police were found walking the railway tracks looking for obstructions or signs of sabotage or damage, incidentally the same job that their predecessors did nearly 100 years before.

On 11th May 1926 the TUC led by Mr J.H. Thomas called off the strike and most of the striking workers made their way back to work. The miners continued until November 1926 but they then were literally forced back to work for longer hours and less money, the strike had gained the miners absolutely nothing.

In 1935 polices establishments through the railway companies increased, the Southern Railway transferred existing employees into the police on secondment and if they were found suitable they would transfer and be appointed as a full time railway policeman. The London, Midland and Scottish Railway preferred to recruit ex-servicemen.

The London and North Eastern Railway began to train all their new police recruits by sending them to the Metropolitan Police training centre in Hendon or other established police training centres throughout the country, this was in order to train and work with local police constables as they believed by training with local constables it would make the railway police more professional and of course more disciplined.

This was the exception to the rule because most new police recruits were given a copy of the police Manual of

Guidance and told to attend all the lectures given by the police in their own time in other words get on with it.

But while all this took place something's never changed in the life of a railway policemen and that was murder on the railway.

CHAPTER NINETEEN

THE TRAGIC PETER RAMPSON

It was September 1938 when the 4.45am parcels train from Waterloo Station was running between Putney and Barnes Stations, when passing a spot on the line known as Dryburgh Road Bridge, the driver of the parcels train noticed something what appeared to him to be a white bundle or something lying between the up line and the down line.

He decided to stop at Barnes Bridge Station and he reported the matter to the staff on duty and they in turn informed the staff at Barnes Station who immediately sent someone down the track to where it was said the white bundle was. The station foreman found the bundle and it was in fact the body of a male child clothed in just a white vest and it appeared that death had taken place many hours before.

The foreman having made the discovery left the body there and immediately informed both the railway police and the 'V' division of the Metropolitan Police.

The body was removed to the local mortuary and the Kingston District Railway Police, Detective Sergeant Redding and Detective Constable Smith were sent to investigate the crime along with the officers from the Metropolitan Police.

This is where the railway police came into their own with one pertinent question, were there any burns on the body and upon being informed that the right buttock and arm were slightly burned, then enquiries could be made to establish what time the electric current on the lines was turned off. It was established that the current was switched off at 1.45am. If as the enquiry suggested the body of the child was thrown from a train onto the track then it could be only one of three trains.

The last train on the up line was the 10.33pm from Barnes Bridge Railway Station and upon questioning all the staff there it was elicited from them that they do remember a woman carrying a child that got on the train to go to Vauxhall.

On 18th September 1938 a man and a woman who kept a boarding house in Vauxhall Bridge Road walked into Rochester Row Police Station and they told the police that one of their lodgers, a Marguarita Eastwood had on one day was seen with a baby and the next day was seen without the baby, and when they enquired she told them that the baby was with foster parents in the Caterham area.

Immediate enquires were made in that area and Miss Eastwood was found and taken to Putney Police Station. In interview she said that the child Peter Rampson was the illegitimate offspring of her husband, who was a soldier and a prostitute he had been with, the husband being in the Grenadier Guards had failed to support the child and the prostitute did not want it.

So Eastwood took the child but in desperation owing to the fact that she was unemployed, she went for a walk and got on a bus to Barnes Bridge then she went to the station and bought a ticket for Vauxhall, when in the train it was her intention to drop the child out of the window, and in she fact held the child at the open window at least three times but could not do it, but then all of a sudden the train lurched and the child fell from her grip and out of the open window and onto the ground next to the track.

This story was not to be believed and Mrs Eastwood was charged with murder of the young child Peter Rampson, and she stood trial at the Central Criminal Court where the jury returned a verdict of guilty of murder and the sentence of death was passed upon her.

This was later commuted to penal servitude for life.

The railway police officers concerned in this enquiry and the obvious delicate investigation were commended for their work by the Commissioner of Police for the Metropolis.

CHAPTER TWENTY
THE SECOND WORLD WAR AND THE RAILWAYS

The Second World War began on 3rd September 1939 when Germany invaded Poland and it was to last for six years until 1945 and in this time the strength of the railway police doubled from its pre-war numbers.

With many men conscripted to the war effort, special constables and female officers were employed again only on this occasion the female officers were to stay as part of the ever growing railway police.

Virtually all the railway police were now trained in the use of firearms by this time and many particularly those officers working at the docks and the ports carried firearms all of the time.

During enemy bombings on the UK, railways were always a favourite for the Germans to attack, as of course the railway would not only carry supplies to where the troops were based in the UK, they would also carry the troops themselves. So inevitably railway stations, railway lines and trains often took direct hits from the enemy bombs.

In London 79 of the underground stations were used as air raid shelters by members of the public during the war when the enemy aircraft flew over London, but despite this there were still some serious incidents and unfortunately this led to many deaths.

Balham Underground Station was one such deep tube station that was used as an air raid shelter and on 14th October 1940, a 140kg semi armour piercing fragmentation bomb fell on the road above the northern end of the platform tunnels causing a large crater.

The northbound platform tunnel partially collapsed and was filled with water and earth from the fractured water pipes and sewers above, this caused an horrendous flow of water and debris which went as far as the southbound platform tunnel, and this caused the deaths of some 68 people, men women and children, who were in the underground station sheltering from the bombs, more than seventy people were reported injured.

The Railway Police

On 11th January 1941 at Bank Underground Station 57 people died and 69 were injured when a German bomb hit the central line ticket office, the bomb left a crater that measured 120 feet by 100 feet and the bomb caused the station to be closed for two months.

On 3rd March 1943 at Bethnall Green Underground Station the air raid siren sounded and people were beginning to make their way down the flight of steps into the underground booking area, but this time it was not the German bomb that caused the deaths.

An anti—air craft battery being used by the British army which was in Victoria Park a few hundred yards away, launched a salvo of anti-air craft rockets, this kind of noise was new to the public and of course they panicked and began running down the flight of steps, it appears that someone fell over or slipped over and others just carried on running literally causing other people to fall on top of one another.

Within seconds 300 people were crushed in the tiny stairwell, 172 men, women and children died at the scene and a further one died in hospital making a total of 173 deaths, and over 130 people were injured.

The most tragic aspect of this accident is that 62 of the dead were children.

Other underground stations throughout London suffered damage and there were other deaths but nothing of the scale of the above disasters.

There was also wide spread thefts from the trains and railways during the war which the railway police found difficult to detect, because a lot of the thefts of course happened during the blackouts. Railway police vigilance at the railway owned docks of Southampton, Grimsby, Hull and in South Wales were also required as the police there sometimes had to take on other duties on behalf of the war department.

During the war the railways were run by a Railway Executive Committee who then set up a Police Committee formed by each of the chiefs of police. This committee co-ordinated all of Britain's railway police throughout the war and reported back to the Executive Committee.

The need for better training was recognised and in 1945 twelve of the most experienced railway police officers from the four main railway companies, attended a special home office run course for police instructors, this subsequently led to the railway police having their own training school for the first time in 1948.

CHAPTER TWENTY ONE
THE BRITISH TRANSPORT COMMISSION

The British Transport Commission (BTC) was created by the Prime Minister, Mr Clement Attlee's post war Labour Government as part of his nationalisation programme, it was to oversee railway, canals and road freight transport throughout Great Britain.

The BTC came into operation on 1st January 1948, and one of its main holdings were the railway networks and assets of the Big Four railway companies plus 55 other smaller railway undertakings, 19 canal undertakings and

246 road haulage companies as well as the work of the London passenger transport board.

On 1st January 1949, the British Transport Commission Police was formed and this was created by using the four railway companies police, the canal police and several dock police, at the time of the re-organisation the BTCP had a police establishment of 3,890 police officers making it the second largest force in the country behind the Metropolitan Police, at this time the London Transport Police consisted of just 100 officers but they did amalgamate into the BTCP in 1960.

The new force enjoyed better pay and conditions but the pay was still lower than the civil police, but perhaps due to the fact that the BTCP were still retaining some of the old railway duties like gate duties and sealing, locking and unlocking goods wagons.

In 1957 an arbitrator granted pay parity with the civil police, this of course made a large force, the second largest in the country even more expensive to run and so the British Transport Commission set up an enquiry to establish whether there was a need to maintain a separate force to police the railways and docks, and could not the civil police, police the railways as well.

The Maxwell-Johnson enquiry found that the police requirements of the railway could not be met by civil forces and that it was essentially a specialist police role, so the railway police or as they were now known the BTCP must remain.

The Chief Constable of the BTCP, Mr Arthur C West had replaced Colonel N McNaughton-Jesper in 1958 and he had made many good and efficient changes to the BTCP including the establishment of the first Force Headquarters, in Park Royal, North London, he completely reorganised the Criminal Investigation Department appointing a Chief of Police (Crime) and based them at the new Force Head Quarters and his new CID would deal with the investigation and detection of crime only.

1961 was a particularly bad year for the BTCP when again they began to fall behind in the pay with the civil police, and as the BTCP were becoming fully trained as police officers many were being lost to other civil forces, it was natural they were leaving for better paid jobs with the many civil forces.

It was no better when soon after the railways were made subject of the 'Beeching cuts' where railway lines were closed and not used anymore and railway stations were also closed, all in a bid to save the country money and in particular save the labour government money.

So less railway lines and railway stations meant less railway police was needed, so very quickly the establishment of the BTCP was down to its lowest for many years at 2,300 staff and morale was at rock bottom.

By the late 1950's the British Transport Commission was losing money and was in a desperate state with serious financial difficulties, and was heavily criticised as an overly bureaucratic system of administering transport services and it had failed to work.

A decision was made by the Prime Minister, Mr Harold Macmillan to abolish it and despite several attempts to split up the transport police but with special thanks to the Railway Federation and their hard work and dedication, this act was thankfully prevented and they remained.

On the 1st January 1963, the word commission was dropped and the British Transport Police or BTP were now born.

CHAPTER TWENTY TWO
THE MURDER OF A RAILWAY EMPLOYEE

Before the BTCP was abolished they were involved in a murder investigation where an employee of British Rail was murdered. In the early part of August 1952 the BTCP played its part in a very successful murder investigation led by Superintendent John Shearing who was a senior police officer with the Great Western Railway Police.

Geoffrey Charles Dean was 28 years old and lived with his wife and small child in Aldershot. He was employed as a booking clerk at Ash Vale Railway Station and had been there for 15 months.

On Friday 22nd August 1952 he was brutally murdered in the booking office where he worked and he had been stabbed in excess of 20 times for the sum of £160, because that's exactly how much had been stolen.

The murderer was a young man called John James Allcott, he too was married and he was a 23 year railway fireman from Hither Green Depot, London, he had commenced his annual leave on the Monday before the murder and had told his wife he was calling in at work to collect his holiday pay as they were proposing to go to France. He left but did not return and that was the last his wife was to see off him prior to his arrest.

Allcott travelled to the Aldershot area and stayed the Monday night at a hotel and one of the first things he did was to purchase a sheath knife, one assumes he was planning some sort of robbery. He was seen at Ash Vale Railway Station several times leading up to the murder, and on the Thursday 21st August he actually went into the booking office and showed the booking clerk his railway pass and asked to use the telephone. He left but returned later the same evening where he spent some time talking with the booking clerk until the office shut at 8.00pm.

It appears that Allcott had been hanging round Ash Vale Railway Station for most of that day and he was seen speaking to several employees of the station.

The Railway Police

On the day of the murder Allcot again went to the station and was first seen in the booking office at 6.30pm then at 7.30pm when Geoffrey Dean was on duty. The booking office normally closed at 8.00pm and any tickets issued thereafter would be issued from the waiting room, Mr Dean gave the tickets and date stamps to a senior porter and told him although the office was locked he was working late on some accounts that he needed to finish before he went home.

Allcott was still in the office with Mr Dean and both were seen by the senior porter who of course was the last person apart from the murderer to see Mr Dean alive.

The murder was discovered at 8.55pm that night when a junior porter saw a light on and he mentioned this to another porter, thinking that something might be wrong he then decided to climb onto the window sill and looked through the window and could he see the legs of a man lying in a pool of blood, he could also see that the safe door was open.

The Station Master was called and he forced the office door open and saw the body of Geoffrey Dean lying on the floor, face upwards covered in blood and also there was blood on the floor. The office safe was wide open there was some papers on the floor with a bunch of keys and some copper coins.

The police were called and in a short space of time the local police along with the railway police were soon in attendance at the scene of the murder.

A waiting room at the station was used as a temporary police incident room and one of the first lines of enquiry that the police did, was to check all local hotels and lodging houses, a normal thing to do in such a murder investigation.

On the Saturday morning the day after the murder, two officers visited a house in Victoria Road, Aldershot as they were aware that the owner occasionally took in lodgers, and they were showed to a first floor bedroom and on entering this room they saw a blood stained jacket, inside was a blood stained wallet containing a British pass port and two 10/—notes.

They informed the Superintendent and the two officers remained at the house to see if the lodger returned to the room.

At 11.15pm that night some 26 hours after the murder of Mr Dean, Allcott returned to the room and was arrested, he was searched and over £109 in cash was found on him, he immediately made a statement to the officers implicating himself and told them where the knife was, which had been hidden in the chimney in the room.

Allcot had been in Aldershot all that day and had bought himself some new clothes to replace the blood stained clothes which were all found after a persistent search by the police.

Allcot was duly charged with murder of Mr Dean and stood trial at Surrey Assizes on 18th November 1952 where he was found Guilty and sentenced to death; he was hanged on 2nd January 1953.

This was a case where both the local police and the BTCP worked hand in hand to secure the evidence, the arrest and conviction of Allcott.

CHAPTER TWENTY THREE

THE GREAT TRAIN ROBBERY

On 1st January 1963, the BTCP became known as the British Transport Police, or BTP as they are still known today, the word commission was dropped from its title and it was not long until the newly formed BTP were called into action because on Wednesday 7th August 1963, one of the most audacious robberies took place and it was the infamous 'The Great Train Robbery'

Late on that Wednesday night the, 'Up Special Train' as it was referred to left Glasgow Central Station on route to London Euston, the train was described as a TPO or

Travelling Post Office, basically it consisted of a number of carriages where post office staff sorted the mail and parcels prior to its arrival at Euston Railway Station.

The second carriage from the front of the train was known as the HVP or High Value Package, that's where the registered mail was sorted and most of it consisted of cash, on this particular day which was a Bank Holiday in Scotland it was estimated that there was between £2.3 and £2.6 million pounds in that carriage (probably in the region of £40 million pounds value today)

Just after 3.00am the driver Mr Jack Mills stopped the train at a red signal, in a place called Ledburn better known as 'Sears Crossing' near to Leighton Buzzard. The green light had been covered and a six volt battery had been used to power the red light.

Mr Mills's co-driver climbed down from the train to ascertain what the problem was and to contact the signal man from the track side telephone. He found that cables had been cut and upon returning to the train he was immediately attacked by someone and violently thrown down the embankment.

At the same time a masked man climbed on board the train and struck the driver Jack Mills around the head rendering him unconscious, then other gang members tied up the five staff in the HVP carriage and others in the team uncoupled the rest of the carriages, leaving the engine and two carriages on its own.

The robbers totalling 15 including, Bruce Reynolds, Ronnie Biggs, Buster Edwards, Gordon Goody, Jimmy Hussey, Roy James, Jimmy White, Tommy Wisbey, Roger Codrey and Charlie Wilson now had a problem, they needed to move the train to a place where they could unload the money sacks, so they decided they needed to move it further down the railway line to a bridge, number 127 some half a mile away so with the threat of violence they used the injured driver Jack Mills to move the train, the member of the gang they chose to drive the train could not drive this specific train.

When they got to this bridge the gang removed about 120 sacks of money weighing about two and a half tons and they formed a human chain and passed the sacks down the embankment into the waiting vehicles. They then left the scene and drove down the back roads to their hideout which was Leatherslade Farm which was about 27 miles away from the robbery.

The robbers began now the task of counting the money which was in £10, £5 and £1 notes; the total amount of money stolen was estimated to be in the region of between £2.3 and £2.6million pounds, I do not think anyone knew the exact amount even the Post Office.

A huge police investigation was launched that involved the Buckinghamshire Police, the British Transport Police, but it was led by The Flying Squad from Scotland Yard and the senior officer in overall command was Detective Chief Superintendent Jack Slipper also known as 'Slipper of the Yard,' one of the most famous and brilliant detectives of all time.

The BTP had a small role in the investigation and most of their time was spent conducting the railway enquiries, obtaining lists of staff and possible suspects who may have the requisite knowledge of the area of the robbery or any knowledge of the workings of trackside signals fairly mundane stuff but work that had to be completed.

The original crime report for the robbery was actually completed by a PC Blake of the BTP and it is still held by the BTP along with a cardboard box marked 'Train Robbery-Cheddington' with some hand written notes made by BTP officers who had attended the scene at the time.

The 15 man gang split the money up and left the farm sooner than they wanted to. A nearby resident suspicious about comings and goings from the farm notified the police and a local officer went to the farm. There he found abandoned food and provisions, sleeping bags and bedding, bank note papers, post office sacks and registered mail packages.

The Railway Police

A scene of crime examination of the farm led to several fingerprints being found, and the identification of the fingerprints along with other on-going enquiries led to the arrest of the gang.

In total 13 of the 15 man gang were arrested more or less straight away, but it did take nearly five years to arrest the leader of the gang Bruce Reynolds and very little of the money was ever recovered.

The trial was held at Aylesbury, Buckinghamshire on 20th January 1964 and after a trial lasting 51 days all were found guilty of various charges connected with the robbery, prison sentences totalling 307 years were handed down and some of the gang received sentences of 30 years for their part in the robbery.

The story of the Great Train Robbery does not end there and although we know that two of the gang escaped from prison, one was later re-arrested in Canada and returned to the UK to finish his sentence, and was released in 1978 he then went to live in Spain where he was later shot dead.

The other escapee ended up in Brazil where he lived until 2001 when he voluntarily returned to the UK to finish his sentence and he was released on compassionate grounds in 2009.

A third had a film made about him but he committed suicide in 1994, and another two of the gang have since been arrested for being involved in drugs.

The saddest part of this robbery is that of Jack Mills the driver, he had constant headaches for the rest of his life and died in 1970.

CHAPTER TWENTY FOUR

PROGRESS FOR THE BRITISH TRANSPORT POLICE

The Chief Constable of the BTP Mr West retired on 1st September 1963 to be replaced by Mr William Owen Gay, he had joined the Great Western Railway Police as a constable and had steadily worked his way through the ranks. He was a well-liked man and a prolific writer on the police and on all aspects of law subjects.

The new Chief Constables first job was to improve the morale within the BTP, and this was done by persuading the Police Committee to restore pay parity with other forces and to introduce some sort of supplementary allowance to be paid lieu of the rent allowance currently being paid to the civil police.

He also introduced a special police pension for the members of the BTP thus allowing them to retire younger and having the desired effect of reducing the overall age of the BTP. In 1964 the hours of duty for the BTP were reduced from 48 hours per week to 42 hours per week. In 1968 the retirement age was reduced from 65 to between 55 and 57 for constables and sergeants and 60 for inspectors.

Also the same year all new BTP recruits were now trained at district police training centres to train alongside their civil police colleagues. And towards the end of the 60's decade the working week was again reduced from 42 hours per week to 40 hours per week.

So in a relatively short space of time the new Chief Constable had changed many things within the BTP and all had raised the morale of its officers.

So there was progress still being made after all these years, now do not forget we have traced the railway police back as far as 1826 and here we are over 140 years later and they are still playing catch up with the civil police.

What were the seventies to bring for the BTP? Well probably one of the first noticeable things was that in 1973 police escorts on the Travelling Post Office trains were ceased, these were bought in after the Great Train Robbery of 1963 and every single night since as long as there was a Travelling Post Office train there were railway police on board.

In June 1974 Chief Constable William Gay retired from the BTP to be replaced by Mr Eric Haslam, OBE, he had been the former Deputy Chief Constable of the Kent Constabulary, under the new Chief Constable further progress was made and within months of his appointment equal pay for police women of the BTP was introduced.

He also introduced new technology to the BTP to assist in the recording of crime on the railways, a modern computer system was set up to record reports of crime and the BTP was the first police force in the country to use computers to record crime.

In 1979 the Edmund Davies Committee looked into police pay and awarded large pay rises to the Home Office police forces, non-Home Office police forces like the BTP were not included so once more the pay of the BTP fell behind that of the civil police, causing more unrest and low morale and in fact led to many BTP officers leaving to join the civil police.

The Wright Committee was set up to look into the pay of non-Home Office police forces and thanks to the massive effort put in by firstly the Railway Federation and secondly the Assistant Chief Constable of the BTP Mr

Nicholls, the BTP became the only non-Home Office force to have 100% parity with Home Office forces, it had taken a long time coming but they were now on equal footings with their civil police colleagues.

CHAPTER TWENTY FIVE

THE RAILWAY AND THE PIRA

The Provisional Irish Republican Army (PIRA) has always targeted the railway system and during the 1970's it was going to be no different and for the officers of BTP it was going to be a particularly busy time.

Part of the tact used by the PIRA was to spread fear and panic amongst members of the public, and what better way is there than to plant a bomb in a railway station or even on a train, you can only imagine the widespread panic it caused.

One of the best features of the British public is, if you tell them to look out for something like suspicious packages, parcels or unattended luggage or bags or even people acting in a suspicious manner they will find them, of course there were many false alarms along the way but that was to be expected and nobody including the BTP minded one bit.

PIRA once said *'you have to be lucky all the time we have to be lucky only once'* a very true and daunting message.

The PIRA had targeted the railways in 1939 just before the beginning of the Second World War, they had caused explosions on the railways but when the war started they stopped for some reason, but now in the 1970's it was different British Troops had been sent into Northern Ireland initially as peacemakers.

But on the 6th February 1971 the first British soldier was shot dead by the PIRA in Northern Ireland, he was Gunner Robert Curtis. The soldiers now became the enemy and attacks on them by PIRA were becoming regular and the deaths of other British soldiers were now happening.

That was followed by a day known as 'Bloody Sunday' in the Bog Side area of Derry on 30th January 1972, when 26 unarmed civilians were shot by the British Army and of those 26 some 13 died.

It is firmly believed by some sources that although the British Army initially went there as peacemakers they were now the aggressors so PIRA had to do something to appease their supporters in Northern Ireland.

PIRA decided to bring their war against the British public onto the UK mainland and London, the home of the British Government was also going to be the favoured choice.

When they first started the attacks it was mainly to cause widespread panic amongst members of the public and damage to property. The general public was not intended to get hurt but as their 'war' against the British people continued then it would ultimately lead to death it had to.

On 23rd August 1973 a bomb was found in an abandoned bag in the ticket hall at Bakerloo Underground Station, this was safely defused by the Bomb Disposal officers, a week later another bomb was found at the same station and that too was safely defused.

On 10th September 1973 two PIRA bombs bought chaos to two main line railway stations, the first at Kings Cross where someone threw a bag containing a bomb into the booking hall, the bomb exploded injuring five people. Then fifty minutes later a bomb exploded in the snack bar at Euston and a further eight people were injured.

That day alone Scotland Yard and the British Transport Police dealt with over 100 hoax calls, many of course at railway stations and on the London Underground.

On 26th December 1973 a bomb was detonated in a telephone kiosk in the booking hall at Sloane Street Underground Station, but on this occasion no one was injured in the blast, on most occasions telephone warnings were given but sometimes they were too late to evacuate the people or even too vague as to where the bomb had been left.

On 13th February 1976 a bomb was found in an abandoned suitcase at Oxford Circus and safely defused, and on 4th March 1976 a bomb exploded without warning on an empty train near to Cannon Street and this time there was eight persons injured by the blast.

But the most violent and deadly attack by PIRA on the railways of the decade was to come.

On 15th March 1976, 36 year old PIRA volunteer James Kelly had set out to detonate a bomb at possibly Liverpool Street Station or one of the other busy city centre stations, when just before the rush hour he boarded a train on the Metropolitan Line (now Hammersmith and City) carrying a live bomb inside a duffel bag, he had got on in Stepney Green in the East End but clearly he boarded the wrong train, and he obviously realised that when the train came out above the ground at Plaistow. He got off and boarded an inbound train to head back into the city.

But as the train pulled out of West Ham Station the bomb he was carrying exploded slightly injuring Kelly, he jumped off the train and was being chased by the train driver and a railway guard, he stopped turned round and fired at both of them injuring the guard but fatally shooting the train driver.

When Kelly was finally cornered he turned the gun on himself, however he did not die and was detained and arrested and taken away by the police. He was eventually sentenced to life imprisonment.

On 16th March 1976 an empty train was severely damage by an explosion at Wood Green Station, the train was about to pick up fans from an Arsenal football match but the bomb detonated prior to the train arriving at the station; one person standing on the platform was slightly injured. Three men were subsequently arrested and imprisoned for this attack.

So the 1970's were a particular busy time for the BTP dealing with many incidents that were caused by PIRA, and with the real incidents mixed in with many false and malicious incidents and false calls with good intent they certainly had their hands full.

CHAPTER TWENTY SIX
DEATH ON THE RAILWAY (1)

Two of the most devastating and traumatic things that the BTP deal with are firstly suicides which I will deal with later in the book, and secondly rail accidents particularly those on London Underground, mainly because of the lack of space, also you are in a confined area, the lack of any sort of fresh air, the obvious danger with electricity and the live railway lines and the obvious mass widespread panic of other passengers wanting to leave the underground as soon as possible.

In 1975 London Underground suffered the worst rail accident since the underground was first used in 1863 and as a result of this accident 43 people died and many, many more were injured and forever traumatised.

The disaster is referred to as the 'Moorgate tube crash' and it happened at 8.46am on 28th February 1975, when a southbound train on the Northern line crashed into the tunnel end beyond the platform at Moorgate Station.

The end result was that 43 people lost their life including the driver, they died either from the impact of the crash, injuries sustained as a result of the crash or from pure suffocation because they were unable to get out.

It was the greatest loss of life on the underground during peacetime and the second greatest loss of life on the entire London transport system (the first being the 7th July 2005 terrorist bombings)

The train was the 8.39am from Drayton Park terminating at Moorgate Station but as witnesses have later stated instead of breaking on arrival at the station the train seemed to speed up, now as this was a tunnel end there is a 66 foot overrun and the end of the platform is lit by a red stop lamp, then a sand drag and finally a hydraulic buffer before the brick wall or end of tunnel.

The sand drag slowed the train significantly but it still apparently smashed into the buffer and brick wall at a speed in excess of 40 mph.

The scene that greeted the BTP and other emergency services was utter devastation, all they could see was the twisted mangle of metal that used to be a train, screaming people trying to get out through windows or anywhere that they could from the smashed train, people running from the platform trying to get out of the station all together, and the obvious smell of burning. I do not think any of us could imagine the site that faced the emergency services that morning.

It took 12 hours to release the last of the survivors because of the confined space that the emergency services were working in and the heat and the lack of air, the front cab which contained the driver was so difficult to reach because the rest of the train had smashed into the front cab and horrifically it took four days to recover the poor drivers body.

The cause of the crash was never fully known, some witnesses said that the driver on approaching the platform was sitting up straight and looking straight ahead almost as if he was in a daze or perhaps transfixed with something. Did the driver commit suicide? There was nothing in the driver's life to suggest that he might commit suicide, but no one will ever know what caused the crash at Moorgate, although it would appear it was not a mechanical fault as all later tests on the remains of the train did not show up any obvious faults.

The coroner recorded a verdict of accidental death on all persons.

All the emergency services, fire, police, railway staff and ambulance staff and anyone else that had helped that day were commended by the coroner for their hard work and commitment in difficult circumstances.

CHAPTER TWENTY SEVEN

THE 1980s ON THE UNDERGROUND

The first thing of the eighties that was immediately noticed was the marked increase in violence on the railways particularly on the London Underground, as the underground in particular was a difficult beast to police.

It has over 270 stations, over 250 miles of railway lines and carries almost a billion passengers a year. It is the second longest metro in the world after the Shanghai metro and the third busiest in the world after Moscow and Paris, and it is open for business normally between 5.00am through to 1.00am approximately 18 hours a day, so how do you police that?

In 1980 a Working Conference took place headed by the Home Secretary Mr William Whitelaw and the Minister of Transport Mr Norman Fowler, and as a direct result of the conference there was a government commitment for extra financial resources and this allowed the BTP to recruit an extra 100 police officers, for use on the London Underground not perfect but certainly somewhat better.

Also mobile police support units were established to combat late night violence and vandalism at known trouble spots.

The Chief Constable Mr Eric Haslam OBE. QPM retired and was succeeded by Mr Kenneth Ogram as the new Chief Constable of the BTP.

Two big setbacks happened for the BTP in the 1980's, in 1984 a decision was made by London buses to stop using the BTP to police the buses and the following year the Associated British Ports announced its intention not to use the BTP to police all of its 24 ports of the UK. This was devastating for the BTP as it would mean a massive loss of revenue.

On 13th April 1985 the last BTP patrol officers at Cardiff Docks locked the police station door for the last time and walked away.

Two major incidents happened on the London Underground during the 1980's which led to the BTP appointing an officer to co-ordinate all major incident training for the BTP, and of note the BTP officers have since travelled the country giving inputs on this training to other police forces and emergency services.

The first incident was the fire that occurred on 23rd November 1984 at Oxford Circus Underground Station in the heart of London's shopping district.

The fire started in a materials store on the Northbound Victoria line platform which at this time was being used by contractors working on the station. The fire gutted the Victoria line northbound tunnel the adjacent Bakerloo line platform suffered smoke damage as did the escalator and booking hall.

The probable cause of the fire was most likely a discarded cigarette. Nobody died in the fire but 14 people including a police officer suffered smoke inhalation and went to hospital.

Smoking had been banned on underground trains since July 1984, but the fire at Oxford Street led to a ban on smoking on all sub surface railway stations in February 1985, but nevertheless a very similar incident occurred at Kings Cross St Pancras Underground Station when a passenger on their way out of the station lit a cigarette and threw the match down onto the escalator, the resulting fire killed 31 people.

CHAPTER TWENTY EIGHT
THE KINGS CROSS FIRE

The second major incident to have a massive impact on the London Underground was the Kings Cross fire which broke out at about 7.30pm on the evening of 18th November 1987, it took place at Kings Cross St Pancras Station which is a major interchange on the London Underground system.

The station consisted of two part, a subsurface station on the Circle and Metropolitan line and a deep level tube station on the Northern, Piccadilly and Victoria lines, the fire started on an escalator serving the Piccadilly line which was completely burnt out along with the top level entrance and ticket hall of the deep level tube station.

The escalator on which the fire started was built pre-war and the steps and sides were all made of wood. Although as we know smoking was banned on all subsurface stations the most likely cause of this fire was a discarded match thrown by a passenger, which probably fell down the side of the escalator amongst all the grease and rubbish that had built up underneath the escalator over the previous years.

The fire started below the escalator and spread above it, it then flashed over and filled the ticket hall with flames and dense smoke, and this was not helped by the arrival and departure of two trains which caused a 12 mph wind through the station and straight up the burning escalator certainly adding to the spread of the fire and the speed that it occurred.

In total more than 30 fire engines with over 150 fire fighters, plus 14 ambulances and numerous police from both the Metropolitan Police and the Railway Police were deployed at the incident.

The fire was eventually extinguished at 1.46am the following day and it had left 31 people dead including a seven year old boy and over 60 injured.

Station Officer Colin Townsley from Soho Fire Station was one of the first fire fighters at the scene of the fire and he went down in the station concourse at the time of the fire, he began to make his way back to the exit when he saw a woman in difficulty and stopped to help her, he was later found collapsed at the base of the exit steps and taken to hospital but sadly died of smoke inhalation.

Out of the 31 victims one body lay unidentified for 16 years, he was known as 'Body 115' but in 2004 police using advanced forensic evidence finally identified him as Alexander Fallon a Scot living rough in London.

As a result of an investigation the most likely cause of the fire was a discarded match or cigarette and to date no person has ever been charged in connection with the matter.

CHAPTER TWENTY NINE
THE BTP AND THE 1990s

In the 1990's PIRA began targeting the railway system again, as it had done in 1939 and of course during the 1970's, and at 7.00am on 18th February 1991 they made a general bomb warning for all main line stations.

A decision was made probably by senior officers of both the BTP and Metropolitan Police not to close all of the stations, obviously thinking of the utter chaos it would cause amongst the passengers.

A bomb exploded at Paddington Railway Station where damage was caused to the roof of the building and less than three hours later a bomb exploded in a litter bin at Victoria

Railway Station, only on this occasion one person died and 38 were injured.

Since that date there have been no litter bins anywhere on London stations.

On 29th August 1991 three incendiary devices were found underneath a train at Hammersmith Underground Station they had failed to ignite.

On 23rd December 1991 a further two bombs planted by PIRA exploded one on a train at Harrow on the Hill Station causing damage but no injuries, and another smaller bomb exploded on a train at Neasden Railway Depot, once again damage was caused but there was no reported injuries.

And into 1992 PIRA planted several incendiary devices on trains at several different railway stations in the London area, most were successfully defused but one detonated on a train at Barking Railway Station but caused little damage.

A further problem was the numerous hoax calls that the BTP received and of course some of these were genuine, some completely false and others calls were made with good intent, in 1991 alone the BTP dealt with 1,683 hoax telephone calls and attended at 1,391 suspect packages, each and everyone one needed to be checked out.

The BTP worked long hours during the period of the PIRA attacks to maintain as normal as a railway system as you could under the immense pressure and circumstances.

The Railway Police

On 1st April 1992 under the Chief Constable Mr Desmond O' Brien, the BTP was re-organised into areas each led by an Area Commander, the areas are, London Underground, London South, London North, Wales and Western, North Western, North Eastern and Scotland and at each and every police station there would be an officer in charge, normally at least the rank of Inspector and his role would be to manage the policing requirements of that particular area.

Also in 1992 saw the Conservative Government led by Mr John Major submit proposals to privatise the railway and this quite naturally led to questions being asked about the future of the BTP, this government and successive governments have assured the BTP that it, the BTP would always remain the natural police force for policing the railways.

1994 saw the opening on the Channel Tunnel, also informally known as the 'Chunnel' it is a 31.4 mile long undersea rail tunnel linking Folkestone, Kent with Coquelles, Pas-de-Calais in Northern France that is beneath the English Channel, and who has to police the UK side of the tunnel but also be ready to go the French side of the tunnel when required, yes the British Transport Police.

The have now set up a dedicated group of officers to police the international link to the continent I presume being able to speak French is an advantage.

The mid nineties also saw the BTP increase their civilian workforce to take over many of the non-police roles, previously done by police officers thus allowing the police officers to continue to deal with the more serious side of policing.

In 1996 to assist the increasing pressure on the BTP the force began to appoint special constables once more.

CHAPTER THIRTY

RAIL ACCIDENTS IN THE 1990s

The nineties and in particular towards the end of the nineties bought with it four of the worst rail accidents on the rail network, and this of course put the BTP right into the front of the public arena, the BTP worked long hours on all the sites of the accidents and in the aftermath of the long and complex investigations and to this end the BTP was quite rightly acknowledged by Her Majesty, the Queen and the then Home Secretary.

On 19th September 1997 an accident occurred on the Great Western main line at Southall, West London the result was that seven persons died and 139 were injured. It happened when the 10.32am from Swansea to Paddington and operating with a defective automatic warning system went through a red signal and collided with a freight train leaving its depot.

The automatic warning system (AWS) and as it was purely an advisory system and at that time it did not have to be switched on, as in this case it was faulty so the driver had turned it off.

The passenger train driver in this case was originally charged with manslaughter after a lengthy investigation but the case was dropped by the Crown Prosecution Service.

On 5th October 1999 the Ladbrooke Grove rail crash also known as the Paddington train crash occurred at Ladbrooke Grove, London, the result was that 31 people died and 520 were injured.

Just after 8.00am on 5th October 1999, two trains collided head on at Ladbrooke Grove junction two miles to the west of Paddington Station with combined closing speed of 130 mph.

On 17th October 2000, there was the Hatfield Rail crash at Hatfield in Hertfordshire, where four people died and in excess of 70 were injured. The 12.10pm a train bound for Leeds had left Kings Cross in London and was travelling at 115 mph when it derailed south of Hatfield Railway

Station, the primary cause of the accident was later given to be a left hand rail fracturing as the train passed over it.

The first two coaches remained upright on the rails and all the following coaches were derailed.

The cause of the accident was put down to rolling contact fatigue defined as multiple surface breaking cracks such cracks are caused by high train loads where the wheels contact the rail, repeated loading causes fatigue cracks to grown causing the rail at a due tine to fail.

The Selby Rail crash occurred in 2001 (previously mentioned) so in a little over four years, BTP had long, detailed and complex investigations into four serious rail accidents.

CHAPTER THIRTY ONE
MURDER AT EUSTON UNDERGROUND STATION

In May 2001 the British Transport Police had a new Chief Constable he was Mr Ian Johnstone, CBE, QPM.

In January 2002 a woman was stabbed to death at the Euston Underground Station and this was to be a significant case for the British Transport Police, it was to be the first ever murder investigation when the BTP were the lead force.

This in fact meant that they were solely responsible for the investigation of the crime and all the relevant decisions that would go with such a complex investigation.

Prior to this case a protocol that had been drawn up between the BTP and Home Office forces stating that the Home Office force would have lead over murder investigations that took place with the BTP jurisdiction, however in this case it changed when the Metropolitan Police agreed that the BTP could take the lead.

So the BTP were responsible for the HOLMES information technology system, file preparation and management of the case, the tracing and interviewing all known witnesses all the way through to a successful investigation and prosecution of the offender.

HOLMES stands for Home Office Large Major Enquiry System and is a backronym for the fictional private investigator Sherlock Holmes; it is predominately used by all police forces in the UK for serious and complex crime.

This case also led to the protocol being reviewed and now matters of murder and of which force takes the lead in the investigation and the prosecution of offenders will be decided between the two respective Chief Constables immediately after the crime is committed.

The circumstances of this case is that a Vaso Aliu was having a relationship with a Marquerite Van Campenhout and had been for about 4 years, until she decided that the relationship was over. Aliu could not except this and began to continually harass her by following her where ever she went.

She had ended the relationship because of his overpowering controlling manner, and she had ended the relationship just before Christmas 2001, but Aliu continued to text her and harass her and follow her. He was clearly besotted with her and would not let go.

She even changed the route she took to and from work and even moved house to escape his unwarranted attention but still he continued. But on the night of the murder the 11th January 2002 she was with her friend, a work colleague who she was now lodging with and for some reason only known to her she had decided to take her normal route home.

Later CCTV footage shows Miss Campenhout and her friend walking along the road and into Euston Underground Station and down onto the crowded platform.

Aliu approached her and started pleading with her to take him back but she kept refusing and insisting their relationship was over, when she refused the final time he went to his coat took out a knife lunged forward and stabbed her in the chest and she fell to the floor, her work colleague went to grab Aliu but Aliu slashed him on the arm, the cuts were so deep you could see the bone in his arm.

A commuter who had just got off a train and had witnessed what had happened tackled Aliu but then he stabbed him in the chest and ran off past his ex-girlfriend who was lying on the floor dying and witnesses have said he stopped, looked at her and said, 'You won't do that to me again.'

Aliu then ran up the escalators to the booking hall chased by members of staff and an off duty security guard, when he got inside the booking hall Alui stopped and stabbed himself in the neck and chest several times and he then collapsed to the floor covered in blood, he did however manage to survive the serious self-inflicted injuries.

The first nightmare for the BTP and the Senior Investigating Officer was to preserve two scenes, the first scene being the platform where the murder had been committed and the second scene the booking hall where the suspect had stabbed himself and this was whilst hundreds of passengers were walking about, arriving and leaving the underground station.

The second nightmare that the SIO had was should he shut down the underground station all together, Euston being one of the busiest in London at rush hour and potentially this would leave nearly five thousand passengers stuck on trains in tunnels and the whole of the Northern line would come to a halt.

The decision was made, he had to shut down the underground station and get the scenes of crime officers and forensics to both scenes as soon as possible in order to carry out their forensic examinations.

The Railway Police

Despite Aliu admitting the crime to witnesses in the booking hall several times nothing was taken to chance. The BTP investigators took over 600 witness statements, held identity parades to confirm it was Aliu and linked the knife to him, the police wanted to prove that the man who committed the murder on the platform is the same man who admitted the crime in the booking hall they wanted to be 100% certain.

It seemed like an open and shut case but they never are and neither was this one going to be as straightforward as it first seemed.

The SIO was proved right just weeks before the case was up for trial the defence put forward a plea of diminished responsibility, it was argued by the defence that Aliu had committed the crimes because he had an abnormality of mind that supported the assertion that he suffered from diminished responsibility at the time of the offences.

Aliu had stated to the BTP, the Immigration Service and doctors that this abnormality occurred because he was an ethnic Albanian who was born and raised in Kosovo and at the time Kosovo was in a war zone and he was being persecuted by the Serbian authorities. Aliu claimed that he and his family had been beaten and tortured by the Serbs and he had been singled out because of his involvement in a subversive group. He also said he had suffered as a child and been abused by various people.

The Senior Investigating Officer took the decision to send two BTP detectives to Greece to interview Aliu's mother about these so called claims that had been made by the defendant. It was the only way the prosecution could check out the claims in the positive or the negative and try and obtain an accurate picture of what truly happened and of course to see if he was lying or telling the truth.

The interview went well with the mother; she totally dismissed all of his claims of abuse and stated that she had no knowledge of his claims and clearly he had made them up. The decision to visit the mother was the right one, they further made checks on his immigration status and although he had stated to the Immigration Service that he was being persecuted and had fled Albania for Britain as he was in fear of his life, this too was found out to be a lie as he had lived previously in Greece for two years before even coming to Britain.

The trial of Aliu went ahead at the Old Bailey and he was convicted of murder and sentenced to life imprisonment he was sentenced to a further 15 years for other offences of wounding rising from the same incident.

An excellent result for the all the staff of the British Transport Police on their first murder investigation where they were the lead force.

The trial Judge at the Old Bailey commended all the BTP officers for their professional approach and commitment in the way that the case was managed.

CHAPTER THIRTY TWO
RAIL COPS

The British Transport Police became famous in 2002, as the television channel BBC 1 decided to make a television series called 'Rail Cops' which was a tribute to the work of the BTP, a sort of fly on the wall documentary on how they work and of what type of work they deal with and get involved in.

I suppose to most people the BTP is one of Britain's least known police forces but with 2,835 regular police officers, 1,455 police support staff, 206 special constables and 337 police community support officers they are the 19th largest police force out of 43 in England, Scotland and Wales.

They police both the railway system both over ground and underground, in England, Scotland and Wales and to give you an example there are 10,000 miles of railway track, 3,000 railway stations and a daily travelling population in excess of 6 million people as well as 400,000 tonnes of freight carried each and every day.

They also police the Docklands Light Railway, the Midland Metro Tram System, the Glasgow Subway and the Croydon Tram link, and they support the policing of the Channel Tunnel.

The series was to concentrate on six particular officers as they went about their daily work and the programme was filmed on location in London, Kent and South Wales.

In their own way I think the general public and television viewer warmed to the six officers and got to know them through the TV programme, and admired their approach to the work which varied from minor damage, children trespassing on the railways, theft of railway property, drunks all the way up to robberies, sexual offences, wounding's, suicides and as we know the most serious crime of all murders.

And one thing that none of us like to think about is suicides on the railway and in particular on London Underground, how does anyone police that, well you normally do not police it you tend to pick up what's left because if someone wants to commit suicide by throwing themselves under a train then you normally cannot stop them.

Suicides on the London Underground are in the norm always referred to as 'jumpers' or 'one under' by the railway staff and that is not in a demeaning way at all its how they, the staff deal with it.

So I think that after the programme and hopefully by people reading this book they will realise that the BTP do a wonderful job policing our railways. So I think that most people will agree that they found the television programme very interesting and I think on average they learnt a lot about the BTP not previously known.

However railways and in particular the London Underground was going to change for ever on 7th July 2005.

CHAPTER THIRTY THREE
7/7

On 7th July 2005 the London Bombings often referred to as 7/7, they were a series of coordinated suicide attacks upon innocent members of the public using the public transport system in London and committed during the morning rush hour.

During that fateful morning four terrorists detonated four bombs three on London Underground trains and a forth bomb was detonated on a London double decker bus. The result was that 52 innocent people and the four suicide bombers were killed and over 700 were injured some very seriously.

The three bombs on the London Underground exploded within 50 seconds of each other at 8.50am that morning, the first exploded on the east bound Circle line, the train was travelling between Liverpool Street Station and Aldgate Station, the second was on the west bound Circle line train having just left Edgware Road travelling towards Paddington Station and the third was a south bound train on the Piccadilly line between Kings Cross Station and Russell Square Station.

The devastation was not finished at 9.47am an explosion occurred on the top deck of a number 30 double decker bus in Tavistock Square, this bus had at 9.35am left its bus stop at Euston Station where of course crowds of people were, having just experienced the underground explosions and no doubt many of those people were now on this bus.

The below is the estimated timeline that the matters came to light for the police, it is not totally accurate but it gives the reader some idea how quickly these things happen, and how little time the emergency services including of course the officers of the BTP many who were the first on the scene of these terrible explosions have to react.

8:50am:

Initial reports of an incident between Liverpool Street and Aldergate Underground Stations, either an explosion or a collision between trains. The reports from the two stations were initially thought to relate to two separate incidents which later of course was only one such serious incident.

8:50am:

Reports of an explosion on a train between Kings Cross and Russell Square Underground Stations, eye witnesses report the explosion appeared to come from outside of the train and not actually on a train.

8:50am:

Reports of an explosion believed to be on a train at or near the Edgware Road Underground Station.

9:28am:

The London tube operator Metronet states that the incident may have been caused by some sort of power surge.

So 38 minutes after the first explosion or collision nobody is certain what has happened.

9:33am:

Report of an incident at Edgware Road Underground Station, reports are that the passengers on a train were hit by an explosion and are attempting to break windows with umbrellas or anything else that they can use in order to escape.

9:46am:

British Transport Police announce there have been more explosions at King's Cross, Old Street, Moorgate and Russell Square.

9:47am:

Explosion has now been heard on a number 30 bus travelling between Marble Arch and Hackney Wick at Upper Woburn Place and Tavistock Square.

9:49am:

The entire London Underground system is shut down until further notice.

So 59 minutes after the first incident a decision is made to shut down the whole London Underground system leaving hundreds maybe thousands of people trapped on trains in tunnels and of course in darkness.

10:00am:

National Grid announces there had been no problem with power surges on the underground system.

This information pointed now towards an explosion of some other kind maybe connected with terrorism.

10:40am:

The first reports of fatalities are being released by the emergency services and a source speaks of at least 20 persons feared dead again no one is saying that it was a terrorist attack.

11:08am:

Bus services are suspended across the whole of Central London until further notice.

11:10am:

Metropolitan Police Commissioner, Sir Ian Blair confirms fears that it is a coordinated terror attack, but appeals for calm, asking people not to travel to London or make unnecessary calls to the emergency services.

This of course is the first indication that a terrorist attack on the public transport system has occurred.

The above time line indicates the very short space of time of the four explosions, and of course the limited amount of time the emergency forces have to re-act to it and the obvious mass panic that would have surrounded the whole episode.

The end result was that fifty two innocent people died, four terrorist died and over 700 people were injured with over 100 having to stay in hospital for a period of time.

The incident was the deadliest act of terrorism in this county since the Lockerbie bombing of Pan Am Flight 103 in 1988 and the deadliest bombing in London since the Second World War.

Although the Metropolitan Police where the lead force into the subsequent investigation into the 7/7 bombings, other forces did assist in enquiries and the BTP were one of those forces.

I have included the 7/7 bombings in the book because I wanted to highlight the danger faced by the BTP in their role of policing the railways and what extraordinary police officers and support staff they really are.

CHAPTER THIRTY FOUR

THE LAW AND THE BTP

As you can see by the previous chapters in the book the railway police have had a varied and interesting history since their beginning way back in 1826.

But what many readers would no doubt like to know is what are their legal powers and how do they differ from all the other Home Office Police Forces.

Legal terminology is to most people fairly boring but you have to write it in its legal terminology to really understand what powers they have and what powers they do not have, and what they can do outside the world of the railway and what they cannot do.

As you have already read earlier in the book the BTP do send their police officers to the Police Training Centres spread around the country, the exact same centres of course used by the Home Office forces, Ministry of Defence Police, Ministry of Transport Police and Police Service of Northern Ireland, so there is no doubt similarities in the use of their general powers to the general powers of other police services.

The general powers of the British Transport Police officers have 'all the power and privileges of a constable' when:

On a railway track, (any land or other property comprising the permanent way of any railway, taken together with the ballast, sleepers and metals laid thereon, whether or not the land or other property is also used for other purposes, any level crossings, bridges, viaducts, tunnels, culverts, retaining walls, or other structures used or to be used for the support of, or otherwise in connection with, track; and any walls, fences or other structures bounding the railway or bounding any adjacent or adjoining property)

On any railway network, (a railway line, or installations associated with a railway line)

In a railway station, (any land or other property which consists of premises used as, or for the purposes of, or otherwise in connection with, a railway passenger station or railway passenger terminal (including any approaches, forecourt, cycle store or car park), whether or not the land or other property is, or the premises are, also used for other purposes) in a light maintenance depot, on other land used for purposes of or in relation to a railway, on other land in which a person who provides railway services has a freehold or leasehold interest, and throughout Great Britain for a purpose connected to a railway or to anything occurring on or in relation to a railway.

'Railway' means a system of transport employing parallel rails, which provide support and guidance for vehicles carried on flanged wheels, and form a track.

A BTP constable may enter a track, a railway network, a railway station, a light maintenance depot, a railway vehicle without a warrant, using reasonable force if necessary, and whether or not an offence has been committed.

It is an offence to assault, obstruct or impersonate a BTP constable.

They need however to move between railway sites and often they have a presence in city centres. Consequently BTP officers can be called upon to intervene in incidents outside their natural jurisdiction. The Association of Chief Police Officers, (ACPO) has estimated that some such 8,000 incidents occur every year.

As a result of the Anti-Terrorism Crime and Security Act 2001, BTP officers can act as police constables outside their normal jurisdiction in the following circumstances and if requested to by a constable or so directed by a Chief Constable.

And I am in no doubt that many of the readers have seen BTP officers conducting enquiries outside the world of the railway system, and possible in their own streets of course if they are investigating a crime and they need to see witnesses then they have to travel outside the railway network, in truth we probably would not notice them, we would just look at them and think there are the normal type of police officer we see every day.

In a lot of cases when BTP officers have made significant arrests, and on some occasions they do have to take them out of the railway environment and escort them to a Home Office Approved Police Station to be processed for the crime that they have arrested them for, as a lot of the police stations within the railway system cannot afford defendant's their reasonable entitlements under the Police and Criminal Evidence Act of 1984 although I am in doubt that is changing all the time.

If you need to read anything further into the various arrangements, then as normal there is a policing protocol in force between BTP and Home Office Forces.

CHAPTER THIRTY FIVE

CRIME ON THE RAILWAY

The British Transport Police Authority was established on 1st July 2004 as a result of the Railways and Transport Safety Act 2003, what the act did was to transfer responsibility for the BTP away from the Strategic Rail Authority and the old BTP committee, which up until 2004 has been jointly responsible for the force to the new police authority.

This meant in real terms the act gave the BTP, a wholly statutory, rather than part statutory and part contractual jurisdiction over the railway network. Of note the BTP is funded by the rail industry and not the normal tax payer.

This meant that the BTP took on a more active role in all investigations particularly involving rail crash investigations but obviously it would include all investigations and in particular those involving serious crime such as murder.

But what of crime and who is responsible for the investigation of crime on the railway network of course the answer to that is the British Transport Police, and of all the crime they investigate, trespass and vandalism are by far and above the most common of all the crimes on the railway network.

Trespass and vandalism on the railway is commonly referred to as 'Route Crime' and it is estimated that the majority of these types of offences are committed by the under 16s.

There are at least 60 people a year are killed by these acts and many more horribly injured, trespass and vandalism is a real crime and people really do die.

Then of course they deal with numerous other offences ranging from simple minor damage, through to drunk, through to violence and through to murder.

As part of the battle against crime the BTP have introduced several initiatives over the years which have included Operation Shied in an effort to reduce the numbers of knives being carried and used by passengers on the railway network.

Operation Shied works hand in hand with the national initiative Operation Portcullis which uses knife arches and drug dogs to assist in the search detection of the knife and subsequent offences involving the knife or any other sharp implement.

Another such initiative was Operation Tremor this was introduced by the North West Area BTP and a local home office force to combat the theft of metals from the railway network, this also paved the wave for the national response from the BTP, with the setting up of Operation Drum to cover the whole of the countries railway network.

Of course this includes the theft of live cables from the railway network and it is one of the biggest operational challenges for the BTP, not only the original theft of the metal or in particular the live cable but with it goes delays in trains, and with that is disruption and passenger dissatisfaction and above all there is the need to replace what is stolen to get the trains moving again.

Other areas of crime investigated by the BTP are serious sexual assaults, robberies and other violent crime. With serious sexual offences the BTP along with Home Office forces use Sexual Trained Officers or STOs as they are called; they are called upon at the first opportunity to secure and preserve the scene, provide support to the victims and obtain statements in relation to the crime.

As with murders and other serious crime it is still quite normal for the Metropolitan Police to be the lead force in the Metropolitan Police area, but more and more now BTP will either assist or take the lead depending on the commitments of the Metropolitan Police and of course the same applies to the other Home Office forces.

Anti—social behaviour is a big problem on the railway network and this would also include trespass and vandalism, well in 2007 the BTP adopted the principles of Neighbourhood Policing, and so far they have 315 police officers and 286 police community support officers as part of their 61 neighbourhood police teams located within the BTPs seven policing areas.

The NPTs are now expected to spend at least 80% of their time in their neighbourhoods, tackling the local priorities and concerns of that neighbourhood. It is more than 85% of their time on the London Underground.

Assisting in all their fight for crime is that more and more CCTV cameras are being fitted both over ground and on the underground railway networks, they are of course a massive deterrent for certain crime and a massive evidence gathering tool for other crimes, so I am no doubt they will continue to increase the numbers of CCTV cameras.

The BTP also have to deal with mass public order offences on the railways, but to the BTP by nature they are somewhat experts in this field because for many, many years football fans had used the rail network to go to different football grounds throughout the country, supporting their respective teams, and in most cases BTP will just put serials of police officers on the trains and they will travel with the fans and hopefully keep the peace.

All their hard work and fight against crime on the railway has in 2009 been supported by the opening of two Force Control Rooms, one at Birmingham and one at London which covers the underground as well and a Force Contact Centre which is in Birmingham, the call centre is responsible for the handling of all routine telephone calls

The opening of these communication and control rooms makes the BTP all the more professional in the way they react to almost every incident on the railways on every day of the week, 24 hours a day, 7 days a week, 365 days a year.

I would like to finish this chapter on a lighter note, there was a theory put forward many years ago that the notorious Whitechapel murders allegedly committed by the now famous Jack the Ripper in the autumn of 1888, were in the fact the work of a railway policeman, who's knowledge of London's over ground and underground rail network allowed the killer to come and go at will, completely undetected, completely without suspicion, and of course of leaving the crimes unsolved forever.

Well what do you think?

CHAPTER THIRTY SIX

DEATH ON THE RAILWAY (2)

Another part of the BTP's less attractive work involves death on the railway and the very unpleasant aftermath that goes with each and every death.

There are about 300 deaths a year on the rail network, most of these death are suicides probably in the region of 90%, other deaths occur on level crossings when drivers or people try to race the train and normally loose, others of course on level crossings where people have quite deliberately committed suicide.

The world of the London Underground has always seemed to be a magnet for people wanting to commit suicide, they seem to think by jumping under a train it is quick and painless, well of course we know that is not always the case as more and more people are surviving suicide attacks particularly on the underground system.

People now know that by jumping under a train can be less reliable than most people have always thought, there is no point of jumping under a 100 ton train and have it go over your legs and crushing them to bits and you are still alive, seems like a pointless exercise to me.

Most platforms at deep tube stations now have pits beneath the track originally constructed to aid drainage of water from the platforms, but they also help prevent death or serious injury when a passenger falls or jumps in front of a train.

This pit also allows the rescuers access to the victim or quite literally it gives them a chance to move the train from above the body or badly injured person without causing more injury or damage to them.

These pits are officially called 'anti-suicide pits' or colloquially known as 'suicide pits' or 'death pits.' Railway staff tend to refer to suicides or suicide attempts as a 'jumper' or 'one under.'

But the impact of all suicides on the on the railway network particularly the underground, on the BTP, the victim's family, witnesses who have seen it and ultimately the train driver himself is most devastating because it has even been known for some drivers blame themselves for not stopping and some drivers never drive a train again, such is the devastating effect it can have.

How do we stop suicides on the railway network? Well you cannot but you must try and at present Network Rail and the Samaritans are indeed working together to attempt to reduce suicides by increasing the training and awareness of railway staff and train drivers, Samaritans poster have been put up on most platforms particularly on the underground with telephones installed on most of these platforms direct to the Samaritans. It may help and if you only help one potential suicide victim it can be deemed some sort of success.

Deaths at level crossing is again almost impossible to stop, you can warn people about the dangers of running across the track when the gates are down, you can put posters up and warning signs and flashing lights but if that person or that car driver wishes to cross the railway track or to take the risk then they will.

Any death on a railway whether by accident, suicide, suspicious or non—suspicious is an area of policing that is most demanding for the officers of the British Transport Police, for two reasons mainly the first being the very unpleasant nature of the work itself associated with the death and the other is the pressure put on the BTP to open the line or platform as soon as possible.

But each death on the railway either over ground or underground in the first instance must be treated as suspicious by the BTP, they have to make an incredible fast assessment as to whether they have a scene, the preservation of that scene or not or can the scene be cleared now or later to allow the trains to run and or the platform to re-open.

BTP is quite clear it will not compromise safety of anyone or of course the dignity of the deceased person. But I think it is fair to say that while we have a railway network we will have deaths associated to it.

CHAPTER THIRTY SEVEN

ROLL OF HONOUR

The British Transport Police National Roll of Honour records the deaths of railway and dock police officers who have died in the line of their duty, in the line of their duty is described as;

Acts of violence

This will include all forms of unlawful killing and includes murder and manslaughter

Misadventure

This will refer to deaths resulting from accidental injury incurred in their performance of duty involving special risks.

Accident

This will refer to death resulting from unforeseen accidental injury whilst on routine duty

Enemy Death

This is death as a result of injuries caused during wartime raids

Death by Natural Causes

This is included if it occurred while performing a particular duty which contributed to the death, includes heart attack whilst chasing a suspect

The British Transport Police Roll of Honour will include all BTP officers and officers from the former constituent forces of, Bute Docks Police, Great Eastern Railway Police, Great Northern Railway Police, Great Western Railway Police, Lancashire and Yorkshire Railway Police, London and North Eastern Railway Police, London and North Western Police, London and South Western Police, London, Midland and Scottish Railway Police, Midland Railway Police, North Eastern Railway Police, Regents Canal Dock

Police, South Western Railway Police, Southern Railway Police, and the British Transport Commission Police.

The role of honour has been obtained from the BTP are it is hoped that the it is correct and up to date, we do understand that the Roll of Honour is a work in progress and that must be taken into account.

There have been many an amalgamation of various railway police forces and for that reason there is no doubt that some records or paperwork associated to other fallen police officers may never be found and may be lost for ever, however it is hoped that other information or records might still be found and the Roll of Honour if not complete it can be added to.

Also to be included in the Roll of Honour the details of each death have to be confirmed and checked against two reliable sources.

The British Transport Police Roll of Honour.

Bute Dock Police.

Police Constable John Scuddamore, died 4th November 1858, aged 55 years.

Great Northern Railway Police

Police Constable William Yellop, died 7th September 1901, aged 26 years.

Great Western Railway Police

Police Constable John Cockwill, died 12th August 1942, aged 61 years.

Lancashire and Yorkshire Railway Police.

Police Constable Alfred Marsh, died 12th January 1898, aged 28 years.

London, Midland and Scottish Railway Police

Police Constable David Tanner Murdoch, died 14th December 1938, aged 45 years.

Police Constable Allan Proudfoot, died 14th December 1938, aged 47 years.

Detective Constable Charles William Bailey, died 21st February 1924, aged 32 years.

Police Constable Leonard Wetherall, died 3rd November 1927, aged 30 years.

Police Constable Peter MacRae, died 15th November 1935, aged 26 years.

Police Constable John Edwin Pyke, died 7th January 1938, aged 40 years.

London and North Eastern Railway Police

Police Constable William Race, died 22th July 1940, aged 52 years.

Police Constable Leonard Percy Bell, died 1st August 1941, aged 45 years.

Police Constable George Edward Barker, died 8th May 1941, aged 65 years.

Police Constable John Francis Woods, died 8th May 1941, aged 52 years.

Police Constable Thomas William Sedman, died 12th September 1923, aged 64 years.

Police Constable George Dodds Whinn, died 28th January 1932, aged 54 years.

London and North Western Railway Police

Detective Sergeant Robert Kidd, died 29th September 1895, aged 37 years

Detective Constable Thomas Hibbs, died 10th August 1901, aged 23 years

South Western Railway Police

Police Constable Charles Ballard, died 30th March 1900, aged 38 years.

Midland Railway Police

Police Constable Ernest Moore, died 4th December 1906, aged 32 years.

Police Constable William Rushton, died 4th May 1912, aged 21 years.

Police Constable Frederick William Loom, died 19th January 1913, aged 63 years.

North Eastern Railway Police

Police Constable George William Leefe, died 26th March 1907, aged 23 years

Police Constable Harold Foster, died 24th December 1907, aged 28 years.

Police Sergeant Henry Bainbridge, died 20th May 1908, aged 34 years.

Special Constable John Arthur Lingard, died 22nd September 1914, aged 29 years

Southern Railway Police

Police Constable Alfred Haynes, died 19th August 1934, aged 40 years.

British Transport Commission Police

Chief Inspector James Daniel McLafferty, died 1st October 1954, aged 57 years.

Police Constable Walter Marshall McMillan, died 25th January 1960, aged 30 years.

British Transport Police

Police Constable Keith Winter, died 23rd November 1970, aged 22 years.

Police Sergeant Raymond George Robinson, died 29th August 1975, aged 55 years.

LEST WE FORGET

EPILOGUE

Well what do you think have I done them justice? Did you know and fully understand what the railway police did and what they were about. I thought I knew as I was a policeman in the West Midlands Police for thirty years and I met many a railway policemen, at various incidents connected with the railway.

But when I set out to research the railway police I was amazed as I am sure you are what they actually did get involved with over the years and I think you will all agree that they deserve our praise and of course support as they continue to do a very difficult job of policing the railway system of the United Kingdom.